Sierra Nevada Adventures

Exploring The Sierra Vista National Scenic Byway

**A Definitive Guide to the
Hidden Heart of the Central Sierra**

Roger & Loris Mitchell

Enjoy the Byway !

Roger Mitchell

Loris Mitchell

Two roads diverged in the woods, and I --
I took the one less traveled by,
And that has made all the difference.

Robert Frost

Sierra Nevada Adventures

Exploring The Sierra Vista National Scenic Byway

A Definitive Guide to the
Hidden Heart of the Central Sierra

by

Roger & Loris Mitchell

Photos by the authors except as noted

Track & Trail Publications
Oakhurst California

Track & Trail Publications
P.O. Box 1247
Oakhurst CA 93644

First Edition 2006
Book design and layout by Track & Trail Publications
Printed in the United States of America

Cover photo: Sierra Vista National Scenic Byway near Jackass Rock

Other current Track & Trail Publications:
Death Valley SUV Trails
Inyo-Mono SUV Trails
High Sierra SUV Trails, Vol. I – The East Side
High Sierra SUV Trails, Vol. II – The Western Slope
High Sierra SUV Trails, Vol. III – The Far North Country
Southern California SUV Trails, Vol. I – The Western Mojave Desert
Southern California SUV Trails, Vol. II – The Eastern Mojave Desert
Great Basin SUV Trails, Vol. I – Southern Nevada
Great Basin SUV Trails, Vol. II – Southwestern Nevada

Library of Congress Cataloging-in-Publication Data

Mitchell, Roger, 1938-
Mitchell, Loris, 1943-
    Exploring the Sierra Vista National Scenic Byway, 1st ed.
    Includes bibliographic references and index
(1) Sierra Nevada Mountains (California) - Guidebook
(2) Outdoor Recreation - Guidebook
(3) History - Sierra Nevada Mountains

ISBN 0-9707115-8-1

This book is dedicated to Mike LeFevre, Recreation Officer
of the Bass Lake Ranger District, without whose years
of work and tireless efforts, the Sierra Vista National
Scenic Byway would not have been created.

The authors and publishers of this guide make no representations as to the condition, drivability, or safety of any of the roads described in this publication. At the time of this printing, all of the road descriptions were up to date as far as was known to the authors. Keep in mind, however, that conditions can and do change quickly, sometimes in a matter of minutes. Be very aware of rapidly changing weather conditions, and use good judgment. Sudden summer thunderstorms can quickly send torrents of water across roads and bring rocks sliding onto roadways. Likewise, travelers in the fall, winter, and spring should be watchful for sudden snowstorms, which may leave you stranded if you proceed.

Common sense would dictate that anyone driving into the mountains, at any time of the year, go prepared with their vehicle in good mechanical condition, and carrying adequate food, water, and warm clothing just in case a breakdown or other emergency should occur. It is highly recommended that drivers should first inquire about local road conditions from the Forest Service Ranger Station in North Fork, or the Yosemite Sierra Visitors Bureau in Oakhurst before leaving. They can advise you of any special fire restrictions that may be in place at the time of your visit. It is also recommended that each driver carry a copy of the current Sierra National Forest general purpose map. Of course, it is always a good idea to let someone at home know where you are going, and when you plan to return. This is particularly prudent in the off-season when there are not as many people around.

Report any emergencies to the Madera County Sheriff's Department by calling 911. However, be aware that cell phone coverage along most of the byway is nonexistent. During the summer months, emergencies can be reported to the Forest Service Clover Meadow Station or to the resident sheriff's deputy stationed there.

Finally, while most of the area described in this guide is on public lands, under the stewardship of the U.S. Forest Service, there are occasionally parcels of unmarked private property interspersed with public lands. If encountered, please respect the owner's rights, and obey any NO TRESPASSING signs that may be lawfully posted.

In summary then: enjoy yourself, but always be vigilant, be cautious, and be safe.

Contents

Acknowledgments

It was Dan Carter, Director of the Yosemite Sierra Visitors Bureau, who first planted the seed of an idea for this guide. His wife Debby, a member of the Sierra Vista Byway Association, added her enthusiastic support and encouragement for the project and, in fact, did much of the creative layout work.

However, it was the people and resources of the Fresno Flats Historical Park in Oakhurst that provided much of the historical content for this guide, specifically Historian Dwight Barnes, Librarian Grace Grady (now Grace Grady-Barnes) and all-around library assistant Virginia Alberta (a long time resident of the area who has enough history in her head to write her own book). Jack Gyer, former historian of Yosemite National Park, and later editor of the *Sierra Star* newspaper, is to be commended for donating hundreds of black and white negatives from the 1950s era to the Research Library at the Fresno Flats Historical Park.

Out thanks also go to Mildred Reed and her son Gary, who made many of the old photos available from the collection of the late Charles Reed. Another North Fork resident helpful in the preparation of this manuscript was librarian and member of the North Fork History Group, Ginny Smith. She kindly gave us free access to the community's historical files. We are grateful for the kindness and assistance provided at the Madera County Historical Society by Dorothy Kenny Foust and Lou Hughes Emmert. Tony Kuret of the Madera County Library also assisted us in our research. National Park Service historian Jim Snyder, now retired, was very helpful in clarifying the National Forest/National Park boundaries before the 1905 change.

We are most appreciative that Debby Carter kindly gave us results of her research on Teddy Roosevelt's debated visit to Globe Rock. Although no conclusive documentation has yet been found, she believes that he did make this visit at some point in time.

We are particularly indebted to a number of folks in the Bass Lake Ranger District of Sierra National Forest who generously gave their time and assistance to us in bringing this book to fruition. In no particular order, they include District Ranger Dave Martin, Public Information Officer Trudie Tucker, Archeologist Connie Popelish, Michael Price, and of course Mike LeFevre, who spent 20 years of his career making the Sierra Vista National Scenic Byway become a reality. Mike kindly reviewed the manuscript and offered suggestions to improve its content.

Our many thanks to each and every one of you!

What Is A Scenic Byway?

There seems to be no firm and hardened definition of just what a "Scenic Byway" is. However, most highway professionals define a scenic byway as a roadway having at least one of the following intrinsic values:

- **Scenic**: Beauty, be it natural or man made.
- **Natural**: Minimal human disturbance of natural features.
- **Historic**: Visual evidence of the past, such as old buildings or other structures.
- **Cultural**: Visual evidence of the unique customs, traditions, or rituals of a currently existing human group.
- **Archaeological**: Visual evidence of the unique customs, traditions, or rituals of a no-longer existing human group.
- **Recreational**: The road corridor itself is used for recreational pursuits, such as jogging, biking, roadside picnics, or direct access to recreational sites such as fishing streams, hiking trails, or campgrounds.

By any measurement, the Sierra Vista National Scenic Byway meets not just one of the six criteria, but five of them! Much of the roadway is both undeniably scenic and natural, as it climbs up along the edge of the San Joaquin River Canyon from the oak woodlands of the lower foothills to the high conifer forests. Along the way, Native Americans have left ample evidence of their having been here long before the coming of Europeans to California. The Ross Cabin and the old barn at Soquel Meadow give today's visitor some idea how the early pioneers lived when they came to the high country. And finally, recreational opportunities abound along the Sierra Vista National Scenic Byway, whether you participate in the Grizzly Century, a grueling 100-mile bicycle rally held every fall, or prefer less strenuous pursuits such as outdoor photography, fishing, picnicking, or camping.

Introduction

The Sierra Vista National Scenic Byway is located in Madera County, on the western slope of the Sierra Nevada just south of Yosemite National Park. The region is about equal distant from the Los Angeles and San Francisco metropolitan areas. Situated between Yosemite and Sequoia-Kings Canyon National Parks, the Sierra Vista National Scenic Byway shares many of the characteristics of its park neighbors to the north and south, yet, because it is little known and only lightly visited, has none of the distracting summertime hoards of people that are found in the very popular national parks. The byway offers bold granite domes just like those in Yosemite. The byway offers a deeply incised canyon similar to Kings Canyon. The byway offers a quiet walk through a centuries-old grove of giant Sequoia trees without the crowds.

While everyone should take the Sierra Vista National Scenic Byway in its entirety, it is not necessary to do the entire 90-mile loop in order to enjoy the natural scenic beauty and unique historic features it has to offer. If you do elect to visit the entire byway in one day, get an early start, and do not plan on taking many of the optional side trips. Taking the byway in segments on different days will allow a more leisurely pace, permitting you to poke along, take the side trips, and better enjoy the country and the spectacular scenery it has to offer. While not everyone will want to take all of the side trips or suggested hikes, there should be at least one that will interest each visitor to the byway. For a more leisurely pace, we suggest the following itinerary:

Day #1: Take the scenic byway from North Fork to the Grizzly Meadow Road. Here you can leave the byway by taking this bypass over to Beasore Meadow, and returning via the Beasore Road (Forest Highway 7) to Bass Lake, then on to either North Fork or Oakhurst. This segment involves 36 miles of byway, exclusive of the side trips. (It is also possible to stay at Bass Lake.) In this day's itinerary you would have time to do the following:

Side Trip #1 to the Exact Center of California Monument (5 extra miles)
Stop #1 - see the Sierra front country from the Redinger Overlook
Side Trip #2 to Mormon Jimmy's cabin and mine (2 extra miles)
Stop #2 - see the historic Jesse Ross Cabin
Stop #3 - see the spectacular view from Mile High Vista.

Day #2: Starting from either North Fork or Oakhurst, take Forest Highway 7 (Beasore Road) from Bass Lake via Cold Springs Summit to the Grizzly Meadow Road. Here you can turn right and pick up the byway again where you left off after the first day. Some 36.4 miles of the scenic byway could now be enjoyed, including:

Side Trip #4 down to Mammoth Pool and dam (12 extra miles)
Stop #4 - Arch Rock
Side Trip #5 to the Clover Meadow Area (8 extra miles)
Stop #5 - Jackass Meadow
Stop #6 - Portuguese Creek
Stop #7 - Globe Rock and bedrock mortars
Stop #8 - Cold Springs Summit
Refresh yourself at Jones Store at Beasore Meadows, before taking Forest Highway 7 back down to Bass Lake (Side Trip #11), and going on to either Oakhurst or North Fork.

Day #3: Starting at either North Fork or Oakhurst, return to Bass Lake and go up Forest Highway 7 (Beasore Road) to Cold Springs Summit, where a left turn will put you back on the Sierra Vista National Scenic Byway. For the third and final segment you can enjoy the following:
Stop #8 - Cold Springs Summit
Side Trip #7, a pleasant walk to the top of Fresno Dome (8 extra miles)
Stop #9 - Fresno Dome Vista
Side Trip #8 to the P-40 crash site (7 extra miles)
Side Trip #9 to meander the Shadow of the Giants Trail in the Nelder Grove of Giant Sequoia Trees (5 extra miles)
Complete the last portion of the byway by descending Forest Highway 10 to Highway 41 and Oakhurst (Side Trip #12). The total miles from either North Fork, or Oakhurst, and back, including the two side trips would be around 41 miles.

While making your plans however, remember that snow covers about 65 or 70 miles of the byway each winter and spring, and the roads are not plowed. This will limit your visit to the byway from late May to mid November. The good news is that the first 15-20 miles of the byway are usually snow-free and open all year long, (except perhaps a few days or weeks after an unusually heavy winter storm). From December through April it is even possible to visit the Exact Center of California, Mormon Jimmy's cabin, the Redinger Overlook, and even the Ross Cabin. Do not limit your visits to the byway to just the summer months. Spring brings an abundant display of wildflowers to the roadsides. The dogwoods, with their large showy white flowers, can be seen along Forest Road 10 in the vicinity of Gooseberry Flat and also in and around the Nelder Grove of big trees. In the autumn, the fall colors are nice, too. The leaves of those same dogwoods turn shades from pink to crimson. Other trees, such as the black oak and the big leaf maple, also have leaves that turn yellow to pink. The golden fall colors put on by the Quaking aspen can best be seen at the start of the Fresno Dome trail.

4

Most of the roads along the byway in the high country were paved by timber operators in the 1970s and 80s as a requirement of their timber cutting permits. It has generally been well over a decade since the ten-mile section of byway between Clover Meadow and Globe Rock has received any maintenance to the asphalt. Consequently the road has potholes and occasional breaks between the macadam. Nevertheless, if driven slowly and with caution, the road is entirely passable to all vehicles from the modern sedan up to the largest motorhome.

A Word of Warning

When you venture into the mountains, be it on a paved highway or a jeep trail, one must always make adequate preparations and go prepared for the appropriate season and weather conditions. Obviously, winter travel requires more preparation than a Sunday outing in July or August, but even then necessities include a spare tire, together with the jack and lug wrench to change it. Regardless of the season, essential items must include water, food, a flashlight or two, and, of course, extra warm clothing for everyone. A warm August day of 104° in Fresno may see summer thunderstorms that produce hail at Clover Meadow. Conditions in the mountains can change rapidly. While on your outings, always be aware of any rapid changes in the weather, and act accordingly. Don't get caught unprepared in a rare September snowstorm. During the winter months when the San Joaquin Valley is socked in by cold clammy tule fog, many miles of the lower byway can be driven in bright sunshine. By all means, take the byway to wherever the snowline happens to be, but use prudence, and go no farther, even if you have chains or four-wheel drive. Don't make the fatal mistake of one couple who became stuck and stranded in January with their bodies not discovered until April.

Be certain that you have adequate fuel when you leave North Fork. The only place along the byway where gasoline can be obtained is at Wagner's Resort on the side road down to Mammoth Pool (see Optional Side Trip #4). A prepared lunch or dinner and snacks can generally be obtained at Wagner's Resort, as well as at Jones Store, from late spring through early fall.

While we have tried to be as accurate as possible in recording the distances, do not be distressed if our road mileages indicated in this guide vary somewhat from your own. Not all automobile odometers read the same, and even a small difference tends to become magnified over the course of 90 miles. The byway is well marked, and the U.S. Forest Service has posted prominent signs at each recommended stop.

The numerical numbers and names of roads may cause the reader the same confusion as they do local residents and even old timers. In the beginning, a road leading someplace, such as North Fork, was simply called the North Fork Road. Then, in their infinite wisdom at some point in the distant past, someone in Madera County government decided that all county roads should be numbered. Furthermore, all East-West roads would henceforth become "Avenues," while all North-South ways of travel would remain "Roads." This method, it was reasoned, would facilitate the assignment of five digit street numbers.

The system worked reasonably well on the valley floor, but not in the mountain area, with its thoroughfares that twist and wind with every hill and valley. In those days, however, what was good for the valley had to be good for the sparsely populated mountain areas as well. So, like it or not, the system stands. Live with it mountain people!

As a result, the county road designations in the mountainous areas are totally without logic or reason. To compound this confusion is the U.S. Forest Service road designation system. Hence today, the last portion of the Sierra Vista National Scenic Byway is officially known as Madera County "Road 632" or " Sky Ranch Road" or "Forest Road 10"!

In 2005, the county supervisors decided to enter a transition period, wherein all county roads in the mountain areas would gradually drop their numerical designation in favor of an actual road name. Over time all road signs will be changed to initially reflect both designations, with the numbers eventually being dropped completely. In our text, we will use both names and numbers for a county road, and the designated Forest Road number for areas within Sierra National Forest.

Report any emergencies to the Madera County Sheriff's Department by calling 911. However, remember that cell phone coverage along most of the byway is nonexistent. During the summer months, emergencies can also be reported to the Forest Service Clover Meadow Station, who can contact the local sheriff's deputy by radio.

Enjoy yourself, but be aware and be safe.

Eastward, beyond the surf of the Pacific, beyond the rolling Coast Range and the wide central valley of California, rises the great wall of the Sierra Nevada. Four hundred miles long, seventy-five miles wide, ten to more than fourteen thousand feet in height, it ranks with the major mountain ranges of the world. Certainly it is one of the most beautiful. Geologically, it is a tilted block of the earth's crust – a long, continuous slope fronting the west, and a short, breathtaking decline to the eastern deserts.

Truly the "Range of Light," as John Muir defined it, the Sierra Nevada rises to the sun as a vast shining world of stone and snow and foaming waters, mellowed by the forests growing upon it and the clouds and storms that flow over it.

Ansel Adams, 1938

Sierra Vista
National Scenic Byway

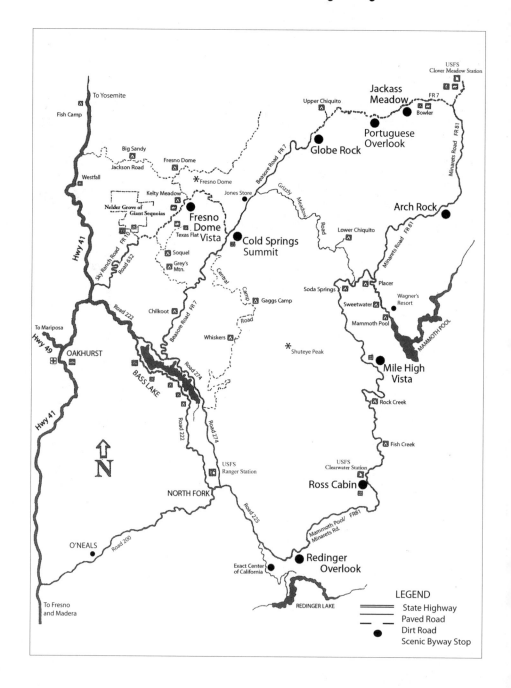

Part 1

Getting to the Scenic Byway

Accessible all year long

Our adventure along the Sierra Vista National Scenic Byway begins in downtown North Fork, California. While most California residents may never have heard of North Fork, much less ever been there, the community is very centrally located in the state and easy to get to if you are coming from either Northern or Southern California.

For those coming from the south:

For those coming from Southern California or the southern part of the San Joaquin Valley, take Highway 99 north to Fresno. Leave Highway 99 at the southern edge of Fresno, taking State Route 41 north in the direction of Yosemite National Park. The turnoff from Highway 99 onto Highway 41 is well marked with "Yosemite" signs.

Highway 41 is all multilane freeway as it goes through Fresno, a city of some 450,000 inhabitants. Fresno's beginnings go back to 1872 when it was little more than a siding and whistle stop. At that time the nearest town was at Millerton, the county seat. The presence of the railroad coupled with the developing agriculture gave Fresno the advantage. Millerton withered on the vine, and an election in 1874 moved the County Seat to Fresno. A grand domed Courthouse was built, and Fresno became the commercial and cultural center of the central San Joaquin Valley.

The original Fresno County Courthouse was demolished
in the name of "progress" in 1966.

Originally, Fresno's streets were laid out parallel to the railroad, in a northeast–southwest and northwest–southeast direction. As the city grew, mostly to the north, the City Fathers decided to change that pattern to a north-south, east-west grid. The first street in this new system was Divisadero. In 1911 the Fresno Normal School, a two-year teacher's college that was to become Fresno State College (California State University Fresno) was built at the edge of town just north of McKinley Avenue.

By 1922, the Sugar Pine Lumber Company had set into motion a grandiose plan to cut timber in the mountains east of Bass Lake. The Minarets and Western Railroad would bring it by rail to a large mill that would be built on the south bluffs of the San Joaquin River, a few miles north of Fresno. A 4½-mile long spur track would connect the mill with the nearest Southern Pacific tracks. The mill would employee up to 600 workers. A separate developer would plat streets and lots, and sell homes to those workers. This new town was to be named "Pinedale," after the commodity they were processing.

Pinedale in its infancy
(Madera County Historical Society photo)

The mill operated from 1923 until the Great Depression years. In 1931 the mill was closed, and the people of Pinedale suffered. When President Roosevelt ordered the internment of tens of thousands of people of Japanese ancestry in 1942, the old lumber yards at Pinedale were used as an "assembly center" to hold internees, while more permanent camps were being built in remote parts of the western states. At that time, thousands of acres of fig orchards separated the City of Fresno from Pinedale. In 1958 Fresno State College was moved from its original location near McKinley Avenue to a new campus well beyond the northern edge of Fresno. Soon, Fresno expanded ever northward, completely swallowing up Pinedale. The only vestiges left today are the half a square mile of old mill workers' homes and the old water tower. Replacing everything else are luxury car dealerships and upscale office suites along North Palm Avenue. Curiously, however, the residential area of old Pinedale still retains its 93650 postal Zip Code, while the rest of Fresno all around it has a 93704, 93711, or 93720 Zip Code.

At the north edge of Fresno, a modern freeway bridge spans the San Joaquin River. This bridge is relatively new, completed in the late 1990s to bypass the older 1938 two-lane bridge on the right. The very first bridge to span the river here was built prior to 1900. It was a swinging bridge held up by cables. The drivers of horse-drawn wagons had to very carefully coax their animals over the swaying bridge, so that they would not become spooked. With the coming of the horseless carriage after the Turn of the 20th Century, the old swinging bridge was replaced by "Lane's Bridge," a more substantial structure made with iron girders. When it was washed out in the flood of 1937, the concrete bridge that can still be seen next to the modern freeway bridge replaced it.

Today the once mighty San Joaquin River is now tamed (some say "spoiled") by a series of four dams upstream. The second dam to be built on the river and the largest of these is 319' high Friant Dam, just ten miles to the northeast. It backs water up to form Millerton Lake. When full, the lake covers nearly 77 square miles, has a 47-mile long shoreline, and holds 520,500-acre feet of water intended for irrigation purposes. A California State Park and Recreation Area, Millerton Lake is a popular place for boaters and fishermen. Wildlife in the area includes a large population of wintering bald eagles and, during the winter months from December to February, rangers offer special guided boat tours to view them in their natural habitat. You can call (559) 822-2332 to make reservations for this very interesting excursion.

The San Joaquin River below Friant Dam

Prior to the completion of Friant Dam, the San Joaquin River was a fine salmon fishery. Indeed, the San Joaquin River was the southernmost waterway in North America to host a spawning run of Chinook salmon. During the salmon run, old timers living along the river said they were kept awake at night by the sound of thousands of fish splashing over the sand bars.

All that came to an end in 1942. The U.S. Bureau of Reclamation, the builders of Friant Dam, made no provision for "fish ladders" so that the salmon could make their way up the river beyond the dam. Even worse, because so much water in the lower river has been diverted for agricultural purposes in most years since 1942, the riverbed is usually dry long before it reaches its outlet in the San Joaquin Delta near the town of Antioch. In recent years, a coalition of environmentalists and fishing groups have been trying to bring back a minimal flow in the river sufficient to re-establish the salmon. As you might expect, the farmers in the San Joaquin Valley feared that any water sent down the river would come from the crops that they irrigate, thus threatening their livelihood and that of the local economy. Predictably, the matter ended up in court where the case languished for eighteen years. Remarkably however, the matter was resolved early in 2006 with a compromise settlement everyone could live with. Under the terms of the settlement, water will flow down the lower San Joaquin River channel again.

Madera County is entered as you cross the San Joaquin River. This county separated itself from Fresno County in 1893, and its residents have jealously guarded their independence ever since. The flavor of Madera County is certainly rural, with its economic base rooted in agriculture. The county only has two incorporated cities: Madera, with a population of nearly 44,000, and Chowchilla, with a population of 11,000. That is all about to change, however, as developers are poised to build thousands of new homes along the Highway 41 corridor just north of the San Joaquin River. The first step in this process was the relocation of Children's Hospital Central California from Fresno to this 50-acre site in 1998, a 255-bed facility that specializes in pediatric medicine, serving families for hundreds of miles in every direction. The colorful hospital structure can be seen on the bluff to the left as you cross over the river.

Continuing north on State Route 41, the trees on the left along the south side of Avenue 12 are olives, while those to the left farther north are pistachios. Madera County's economy is largely based on its agricultural production. The five top farm products are grapes, almonds, milk, pistachios, and cows. After only almonds, pistachios are the second most valuable tree crop in the county. In recent years the local pistachio crop has been worth $30 to $40 million annually. That may pale to the annual $150 million dollar value of the grape crop, but it is still significant.

The freeway portion of Highway 41 currently ends just before reaching Avenue 12, one of two major east-west thoroughfares in this part of Madera

County. **If you have a trip odometer in your automobile, set it to zero at the Avenue 12 traffic signal.**

Proceeding north on the now two-lane Highway 41, you will soon pass pastureland and vines on the left, with many more acres of vines farther on to the right. Madera County is also known for its wine-grape production (the first vineyard was planted in 1870), and the local vintners association has put together a pleasant winery tour where the products of these vines can be tasted. For more information about the winery tour, see their website at www.maderavintners. com or write to them at Madera Vintners Association, P.O. Box 697, Madera CA 93639.

Prior to the coming of the Central Pacific Railroad in the early 1870s, the major wagon road through this part of the San Joaquin Valley skirted the lower Sierra Nevada foothills, and ran from the port of Stockton south to Millerton and on to Visalia. With the ease of rail traffic and growth of towns along the tracks, traffic on the Stockton-Visalia road decreased greatly. As the tourism industry in Yosemite developed during the latter part of the 19th Century, the road south from Wawona went southwest through Ahwahnee and Grub Gulch to join the railroad at Berenda and later Raymond.

In the early years, there was no direct road from Coarsegold to Fresno Station. That situation began to change in 1925, when a meeting took place in Wawona between state highway officials, various county representatives and the Supervisor of Sierra National Forest. It was decided to build a new all weather highway from the south entrance of Yosemite to Fresno. By 1930 Fresno County had built its portion north to the San Joaquin River, and the Forest Service, using men who worked in the forest during the summers, had built its share from Yosemite south to Coarsegold by completing sections during the winters. It would not be until 1938, however, that the State of California completed the last 25-mile segment between the river and the park. Now for the first time, there was a direct, "high-speed" link north from Fresno to Yosemite National Park and, in its "modern" mode of transportation, the tourist traffic seeking recreation in the Sierra Nevada increased even more.

Beyond Avenue 15, look to the left at the undulating grasslands used primarily as cattle pasture. Old timers in the area refer to this landscape as the "Hog Wallows." To the geographer these depressions are known as vernal pools, because they often fill with water during the rainy season, and support a unique ecosystem. Before the grading of Highway 41 became so sophisticated, the asphalt roadway crossing this area rose and fell following the topography, creating a roller-coaster ride for the motorist speeding along at fifty miles per hour.

After admiring the Hog Wallows north of Avenue 15, when your odometer is reading about five miles, look ahead and to the right at the low grass-covered mesa with a band of oak trees just below the top. A century ago this landmark was called "Jeremiah Brown's Table Mountain" and is shown on some early maps as such. Today most folks simply call the flat-topped mesa "Little Table Mountain." And just who was this Jeremiah Brown? He was an early pioneer to the area who brought his family down the Stockton-Millerton trail in the early 1850s to settle nearby and start a "Way Station," where travelers on the Stockton-Millerton Road could stop, rest, and obtain water and food for themselves and their animals.

As incredible as it may seem, this grass-covered butte was once in the bottom of an ancient river channel. During the Eocene Epoch of the earth's geologic history, a river flowed down through foothills of granite leaving a streambed littered with sand, cobbles, and small boulders. In the 40-50 million years that have lapsed since then, iron oxide and other soluble minerals have percolated down through the old river channel firmly cementing the stream gravel together, turning it into a very hard conglomerate. In the meanwhile, the relentless forces of erosion have worn away the hills on either side of the river channel, leaving the firmly cemented riverbed perched high above the surrounding landscape. Thus, what you see today is what is left of the old river bottom perched high above the surrounding plain. The prehistoric stream channel can also be seen to the east across the San Joaquin River in Fresno County. This "Table Mountain" phenomenon can be seen elsewhere in the western Sierra Nevada foothills, such as at Knight's Ferry in Stanislaus County. However, there the resistant rock is not a conglomerate, but rather basalt lava that flowed down.

Originally called Jeremiah Brown's Table Mountain,
most people today call it "Little Table Mountain."

The extensive grasslands in this area once supported large herds of wild horses, pronghorn antelope and Tule elk, but the great droughts of 1866 and 1877 greatly reduced and nearly eliminated those populations. The vegetation here was very different in those days from what you see today. In the 1700s, the early Spanish padres and their military escorts introduced European grasses and other non-native weeds into California, inadvertently and sometimes intentionally. During the years of the next century, these exotic species thrived and spread into California's great Central Valley. Plants such as wild oats, which once grew to heights of five feet, were pushed out and lost forever. Nevertheless, Madera County's grasslands remain a valuable resource to local ranchers whose cattle forage here. Hidden among the grasses are hundreds of thousands of ground squirrel burrows. These rodents, which can often be seen sitting upright on fence posts near the edge of the road, are a major component of the diet of the sizeable coyote population and that of hawks and other raptors often seen perched high on roadside utility poles.

When your trip odometer rolls over to the six-mile point, you will reach the traffic signal at the intersection of State Highways 145 and 41, known by locals today as simply "Four Corners." Those coming from points in Northern California will join us here. Continue north on Highway 41.

For those coming from the north:

For those coming from the San Francisco Bay or Sacramento areas, take Highway 99 south to Madera. Leave the freeway at the "Central Madera Exit." At the stop sign at the end of the offramp, turn left onto North I Street. Go south on I Street crossing 4th Street at the traffic signal. Proceed south one long block, and turn left onto Yosemite Avenue. Just after crossing the Highway 99 overpass, the old Madera Courthouse will be on the right.

No visit to the Sierra Vista National Scenic Byway would be complete without a stop at the old Madera County Courthouse. The two-story stone building was completed in 1902. County government today has outgrown the old courthouse, and moved into new quarters across the street. Unlike its neighbor immediately to the south, Madera County has not torn down its historic courthouse. Indeed, the Madera Courthouse has been beautifully restored to its original magnificence. The building is now used as a museum operated by the Madera County Historical Society. The old courthouse contains three floors of exhibits that preserve various aspects of life in Madera County over the last 150 years. The museum is open weekends from 1-4:30 p.m. with volunteer docents on hand to answer questions.

The City of Madera's origins go back to September 6, 1876, when a valley rancher donated 1560 acres of land near the Southern Pacific Railroad to induce the California Lumber Company to terminate its 54-mile-long flume here, rather than at Borden three miles to the north. The company needed only forty acres for its lumberyard and finishing mill, located near what would become 6th and E Streets. Soon the lumber company was in the real estate business as well, subdividing unneeded adjoining acreage, and then auctioning off parcels for commercial and residential uses. The town came to be named "Madera," after the Spanish word for lumber. When in 1893 a group of Madera's citizens voted to break away from Fresno County, again "Madera" was to be the name of the new county and, of course, the county seat would be located in the booming lumber town of Madera. The last of the cut wood went down the flume to Madera in 1933, but by that time, the city was no longer a one-industry town. By the Turn of the 20th Century, agriculture was now the economic engine driving commerce in the City of Madera.

The flume of the California Lumber Company as it approached Madera
(Fresno Flats Historical Park photo)

Memories of Madera

Madera County Courthouse shortly after it was built in 1902
(Fresno Flats Historical Park photo)

Yosemite Avenue when there was no speed limit, and horses and buggies
ruled the road taking whatever side of the road they liked.

By 1920 motorists outnumbered the horse and buggy drivers,
and by 1930 one rarely saw a horse or mule in downtown Madera.
(photos courtesy Madera County Historical Society)

18

Going east out of Madera, Yosemite Avenue becomes State Route 145. You will want to follow it for about 15 miles, where you will come to the traffic signal at its intersection with State Route 41. (See pages 12-13 for a description of the agriculture in this part of Madera County, and pages 13-15 for a description of the terrain along the way.) Turn left here onto Highway 41. A sign on the right indicates you are now on the Southern Yosemite Highway.

0.0   Whether you are coming from Fresno or Madera, **reset your trip odometer to zero at the intersection of State Routes 41 and 145.** Soon Highway 41 will leave the flatlands on the floor of the San Joaquin Valley to begin its gradual climb through the lower foothills of the Sierra Nevada.

2.2   (2.2) County Road 208 crosses Highway 41 at the 2.2-mile point on your trip odometer. Originally this part of Road 208 was a segment of the 160-mile long Stockton-Millerton Wagon Road, which, like today's Highway 99, was the principal north-south artery through the San Joaquin Valley during the early Gold Rush days. It was in 1852 that Jeremiah Brown, together with his wife and young daughter, established the Wide Awake Ranch and Way Station just two miles to the west.

The oldest building in Madera County, Jeremiah Brown's house
and stage stop still stands on the Wide Awake Ranch.

On the northwest corner of Road 208 and Highway 41 is a relatively new service station and mini-mart. It replaced an older structure. It all started back in the late 1930s, when Claude Miller sold Shell gasoline here from a hand cranked gravity flow pump. Being at the intersection of County Road 208 and the newly opened Highway 41, the place was known as Millers Corner. Miller also sold sandwiches and beer to travelers en route between Fresno and the mountains. After World War II, nearby rancher Francis Leroy Brown, the great-grandson of the previously mentioned Jeremiah

Brown, bought the property and renamed it Sweetwater Station. Brown not only continued the practice of selling gasoline, beer, and sandwiches (his specialty of fresh made chicken sandwiches were often sold out by noon), but he also sold ice, no mean feat considering the fact that there was still no electricity in the area. It required him to drive to an icehouse in Fresno to fill his pickup with a thousand pounds of ice several times a week. The Browns in turn sold the business to one Charles Rogers, the proprietor of a cigar shop in downtown Fresno. Rogers named the place 22 Mile House, because the establishment was 22 miles from his cigar store. Rogers is long gone, as is his roadside bar that was very popular with the motorcycle crowd in the 1950s and 60s. Nevertheless, the name "22 Mile House" survives to this day, even though its present day namesake has yet to celebrate the birthday of its first decade.

On the east side of State Route 41, across the highway from 22 Mile House, the stock pond is fed by a series of small springs. When the state built Highway 41 through here in 1938, little thought was given to surveying the route for possible disturbance to archaeological sites, and salvage archaeology of any sites found if they could not be bypassed. Unfortunately Highway 41 goes through a major Native American campsite here, one that was in use for perhaps several thousand years. A belated archaeological study of the site in 1989 revealed Native Americans had camped here, off and on for perhaps thousands of years. It must have been a good campsite for the Indians. The springs on the east side of the highway provided ample water and tules from which baskets could be made. On the west, the valley grasslands were teeming with deer, antelope and elk. Just to the north, the oaks provided a reliable crop of acorns year after year. The archaeologists discovered stone projectile points that suggested the use of the atlatl, a spear-throwing device in use 2,000 years ago, before the invention of the bow and arrow. Excavations three feet below today's ground surface revealed a fire pit lined with rocks. No charcoal remained from which a Carbon-14 date might be obtained, but a "mano," a hand held grinding stone, was found at the edge of the hearth, just where its last user had left it. The presence of obsidian points suggested these people had trade contacts with other Native Americans from Nevada and the Mono Basin, on the east side of the Sierra Nevada.

As the highway climbs through the oak woodland accentuated by occasional outcrops of granite, the roadsides are a riot of colors in the springtime with large clusters of purple bush lupine *Lupinus*, a ground cover of white popcorn flower *Plagiobothrys nothofulvus*, the bright orange of common fiddleneck *Amsinckia menziesii* and the protected California poppy *Eschscholzia californica*, and the bright yellow blossoms of sticky monkey flower *Mimulus guttatus* lining the moist bottoms of the little swales. Unfortunately, summer visitors to the Sierra Vista National Scenic Byway are going to miss this magnificent sight, because by the time the higher portions of the byway are free of snow, these lower hillsides have already turned brown as the soil dried up.

lupine   fiddleneck   California poppy

6.8   (4.6) A sign on the left indicates the entrance to the USFS San Joaquin Experimental Range is on the right. Established in 1934, the Pacific Southwest Research Station and California State University Fresno operate this facility jointly, studying forest, range and watershed issues.

7.3   (0.5) Look for a turnout on the right when your trip odometer reads 7.3 miles. Built of local granite, the water fountain here was fed by a pipe from a spring on the west side of the highway. In the 1940s and 1950s, the water fountain was a welcome sight to tens of thousands of northbound motorists, whose radiators had boiled over after the 1,000-foot climb out of the valley. Fortunately the cooling systems of modern automobiles can handle that climb with ease. The spring has proved unreliable in recent years, so CalTrans has installed a portable water tank here for use by motorists (the water is not potable), although now days it is rare to see any cars stopped here with the hood up.

7.8   (0.5) Carefully merge into the right lane of the two uphill traffic lanes, for we will be turning to the right onto the North Fork Road, also known as Road 200.

8.7   (0.9) Turn right onto County Road 200. Since leaving Fresno some 18 miles back, we have been pretty much going north. We now turn to the east for the next couple of miles.

10.6   (1.9) The small fenced area on the low hilltop to the right is the private family cemetery established on their land by the pioneer O'Neal family, when their one-year-old daughter Lucy died in 1879. Some of their neighbors, ranch hands and local Native Americans are also buried here.

10.7 (0.1) Road 211 (O'Neals Road) turns off to the right. Prior to the construction of Highway 41 in 1938, it connected Fresno Station and Millerton with the communities of O'Neals, Finegold, and North Fork.

10.8 (0.1) The present day Spring Valley Elementary School on the left announces the coming of the small hamlet of O'Neals. Built on land donated in 1889 by Charles O'Neal in order to educate his children closer to home, the original school stood on this same spot.

Spring Valley School in O'Neals in 1895. Left to right are: Mr. and Mrs. Copsey, teacher Minnie Cummings, Charles O'Neal Sr., Charles O'Neal Jr., and Calvin Bigelow (from the authors' collection)

11.2 (0.4) Continue straight ahead on the North Fork Road (Road 200). Road 201 on the left makes a loop through the tiny hamlet of O'Neals. The cluster of structures consists of a post office, the volunteer fire station, the offices of the Ponderosa Telephone Company, and a few homes. There are no other services of any kind in O'Neals today.

While O'Neals may not be much to look at today, such was not always the case. A few hardy pioneers first moved into this area around 1856, when John Gilmore patented 160 acres of land here, and established a ranch and small store that catered to miners working the auriferous sands of nearby Finegold Creek. The name of the community comes from the Charles and Bettie O'Neal family, who bought the Gilmore Ranch in 1878. It is the only community in the entire Eastern Madera County area that has kept its original name to the present. Direct descendants of the O'Neal family still live here.

Shortly after the Turn of the 20th Century, local pines and oaks were utilized in O'Neals in the making of wagons. In 1910, no less than five stage lines were carrying passengers, mail, and freight out of O'Neals, connecting such places as Fresno Flats, Sugar Pine and North Fork, with Madera and Fresno.

The store, blacksmith shop, dance hall
and Charles O'Neal's residence circa 1890
(photo courtesy Madera County Historical Society)

One of those stagecoach operators was Harmon Bigelow. In 1908, his wife Leota obtained by mail order from the Sears-Roebuck Company two of the new-fangled contraptions called the "telephone," and had her son string wires in trees to her mother's house about a mile away. Harmon liked it so much that in 1910 he had wires strung from home to his stage office in North Fork, ten miles away. Soon neighbors along the way bought phones and hooked on to the wires. From those humble beginnings developed the Ponderosa Telephone Company that today serves some 3,000 subscribers in the North Fork and O'Neals area in Madera County, and the Prather-Auberry-Tollhouse area in Fresno County. Descendants of the Bigelow family still run the company, as well as operating Bigelow Farms, an up and coming producer of fine range fed beef.

Stages out of O'Neals

The Bigelow stage office in O'Neals

O'Neals was the hub of several stagecoach routes
around the Turn of the 20th Century.
(Fresno Flats Historical Park photos)

24

11.6 (0.4) Road 201 on the left goes back into O'Neals. Beyond O'Neals, the North Fork Road passes scattered homes and ranches as it gains a little elevation.

12.8 (1.2) At the top of a low rise, the North Fork Road now crosses the divide, and begins a gradual descent into the valley drained by Finegold Creek. This is cattle country, where for the last 125 years local ranchers have grazed their herds. You may notice many picturesque old barns along the way.

Clarkia

Should you pass this way in May or perhaps early June, you will no doubt notice the showy purple flowers lining the banks on the side of the road. These colorful wildflowers are of the genus *Clarkia,* sometimes called "Farewell to Spring," as it is the last wildflower to bloom in the lower foothills.

15.7 (2.9) House Ranch Road goes off to the left. By taking this side road a half-mile, you will come to the Westbrook Wine Farm, currently the only winery in the foothills of Madera County. This micro-winery bottles some very fine claret wines that are available for tasting, but only if you call ahead for an appointment (559-868-3499). If you are interested, you might first look at their website: www.westbrookwinefarm.com.

Beyond House Ranch Road, the presence of many old cottonwood trees and berry bushes on the right defines the watercourse of tiny Finegold Creek, so named for the gold "dust" that was panned here well over a century ago. The trees put on a colorful show in the fall.

16.7 (1.0) In 1947, this "new" bridge over Finegold Creek replaced an older concrete arch structure just upstream. People still stop and pan for gold beneath this bridge. Stop and look at the creek if you wish, but **do be careful to avoid the poison oak!** Remember the old saying: *Leaves of three, let it be!*

Finegold Creek during winter months

Poison oak!

17.4 (0.7) It was in this general area, near the windmill, that the mining camp of Finegold sprang up in the 1850s. History did a poor job of recording the event. We do know that a N.H. Stockton was working the gravels of the creek in September and October of 1850, sometimes making as much as $30 per day. Stockton's activities attracted others, and soon a small cluster of tents appeared on the creek. This would prove to be the first community in what, some forty years later, would become Madera County. The local Indians, and we do not know if they were Western Monos or Chukchansi, did not take kindly to the new wave of intruders. An 1850 letter to Governor McDougal says that the miners had to flee to Agua Fria (near Mariposa) because of a threatened Indian attack. Brief mention of the camp's troubles is made in the July 10, 1852, issue of the San Francisco newspaper *Alta,* indicating that Indian attacks had driven most of the miners off. The miners began to return, however, and eventually their numbers were such that the Indian threat was no longer a problem. Some writers claim that up to 2,000 miners lined the banks of Finegold Creek. By this time, the hamlet is said to have had all the usual businesses of a western boomtown – several boarding houses, three stores of general merchandise, a hotel, a livery stable, and of course innumerable saloons and gambling halls. The main street was several blocks long, lined with wooden buildings on both sides.

As is often the case in placer mining areas of those early days, Finegold had a large Chinese population. These hard working frugal people made a good living where others could not. The Chinatown of several adobe buildings stood at the eastern edge of the settlement.

Even after the gold played out, Finegold's geographic position kept the small community in existence for another thirty years. The hamlet was a day's travel from either Fresno or Madera, an ideal place to stop for the night. Freight wagon traffic kept Finegold alive, as overnight shelter and food for the teamsters and their animals was available here. Indeed, there were still sufficient people in the area to warrant the postal authorities to open a post office in 1881. The arrival of the automobile ended the need for horse drawn teams, and thus the little town's reason for existence. The post office closed its doors in 1907. Today it is hard to imagine that there was ever anything here. The site is on private property now, and sadly little remains of Madera County's first town.

Placer gold was panned from Finegold Creek
as early as 1850, and every year since.

18.0 (0.6) The bridge over Little Fine Gold Creek is crossed, and the road now begins the gradual ascent of what local residents call the "Walker Grade," named after brothers Charles Franklin and James Null Walker, early settlers who operated a store and cattle ranch in the area. James was elected to the state legislature and served two terms as the sheriff of Fresno County in the 1860s. The road up Walker Grade will climb some 1300 feet in the next four miles.

If you should pass this way in late winter to early spring, your attention may be drawn to a multi-stemmed deciduous shrub standing 8 to 20 feet tall with vivid magenta or purple blossoms. You are probably looking at the Western redbud *Cercis occidentalis,* a member of the Pea family. A native of the Sierra foothills, its roots contain nitrogen-fixing bacteria that contribute to the natural fertilization of the soil.

If on the other hand, you see a similarly large shrub or tree having six-inch long clusters of white blossoms, you are then seeing the California buckeye *Aesculus californica*. This native plant of the western Sierra Nevada foothills typically grows 10 to 15 feet high, with a similar width. This deciduous tree is the first to leaf out in the springtime, as well as the first to turn brown and drop its leaves in the heat of mid-summer. The California buckeye produces clusters of showy white flowers in May and early June. By late summer, the leaves have fallen, and pear-like brown seed pods about the size of a golf ball are left hanging from the tips of its branches. Often called horse-chestnuts, they can cause nausea, vomiting and even paralysis if eaten untreated.

The showy white flowers and the seed pods
of the California buckeye

19.9 (1.9) If you have a keen eye and are not going too fast, look across the valley to the left, where you can see a large railroad cut in the hillside, made during the construction of the Minarets and Western Railroad in 1922-23. A captive company of the Sugar Pine Lumber Company, this standard gauge railroad carried timber from Bass Lake to the company's mill at Pinedale, located just north of Fresno. After the Sugar Pine Lumber Company ceased operations in 1930, the railroad was no longer needed. The line was abandoned in 1934, and the last of the rails were torn out in 1939. The 53-mile long right-of-way wound its way across the North Fork Road (Road 200) three times between North Fork and O'Neals.

20.3 (0.4) The right-of-way of the Minarets and Western Railroad crossed the North Fork Road (Road 200) at this point. For steam locomotives of that era, this was a fairly steep grade of 2½%. Fortunately, the heavily laden trains were going downhill. The rail cars were mostly empty on the return trip up the hill.

20.7 (0.4) The California Department of Forestry and Fire Protection's Rancheria Fire Station on the right is staffed with two wildland fire engines, each with three firefighters on board, during the May-October fire season. Only one person is on duty the rest of the year. Campfire permits valid in the national forest are available here at no cost.

22.1 (1.4) Road 200 reaches the top of the Walker Grade. Having traveled to here in an air-conditioned car, it is hard to imagine a stagecoach passenger in the heat of summer being asked to get out and walk part of the way to ease the load on the horses.

22.2 (0.1) The entrance to the Bass Fork Mini-mart and service station is on the left. This is the first opportunity to obtain a cold drink and a snack since leaving 22 Mile House some 20 miles back.

22.3 (0.1) County Road 221 (Crane Valley Road) starts off on the left towards Bass Lake, just a few miles to the north. Stay on the North Fork Road (Road 200).

25.2 (2.9) We will want to go straight here at the intersection of the North Fork Road and the Auberry Road (Roads 200 and 222). Technically Road 200 ends here, and the road straight ahead becomes Road 222. Do not turn to the right. That is now the Auberry Road (County Road 222) that descends five miles to Kerckhoff Lake, where it crosses the San Joaquin River and ascends the Fresno County side to go into the community of Auberry.

25.5 (0.3) Road 222 now enters North Fork. A sign announces the elevation is 2,640 feet. In recent years the population of this community has remained pretty steady at about 3,500 people.

About 500 years ago, small bands of Paiute Indians from what is now Inyo and Mono Counties migrated westward over the Sierra Nevada to settle here along Willow Creek. Here on the western slopes of the mountain range, they no longer had the very nutritious nuts of the piñon pine, but this shortcoming was made up by the presence of acorns from oaks and more abundant game. The Monos learned from their neighbors, the Yokuts and Chukchansi, and soon adapted to their new environment. (The descendants of these Paiutes make up the North Fork Rancheria. They show off their cultural heritage at the Sierra Mono Indian Museum on County Road 228 near its intersection with Road 225, just east of downtown North Fork.)

There was no seminal moment in history when North Fork began. It is sometimes said that while it was gold that first brought the white man to North Fork, it was timber that caused him to stay. Gold was being panned in the rivers and streams at Fort Miller (Millerton), Finegold, and Coarsegold in the early 1850s. Prospectors undoubtedly passed through this area as well but, in the absence of gold, quickly moved on. The first road in the area connected Fort Miller (later Millerton) on the San Joaquin River with a sawmill on the Board Ranch in Crane Valley (now covered by the waters of Bass Lake). The first actual resident of North Fork appears to be one Milton Brown, who built a small cabin here around 1865. Brown sold supplies to the few local ranchers and to cattle and sheep men who moved their livestock through the area each spring and fall, and the location came to be known as "Brown's Place." By the mid-1870s, a few more cabins had sprung up, as did a second store and several saloons. The early 1880s saw roads radiating out from Brown's Place in every direction, but particularly to the east where the tall timber could be felled. After the Peckinpah Mill opened in 1881, several other sawmills soon followed. Ox teams were moving all of that cut lumber down through Brown's Place.

In the 1880s ox teams moved cut trees to the mill.

The Peckinpah Mill was one of the first in the North Fork area.
(photos above from the Charles Reed Collection)

In December of 1888, the North Fork Lumber Company exerted sufficient clout with postal authorities to establish a post office, and it would be called "North Fork". It was the year 1892 that saw the first bridge over the North Fork of Willow Creek. It was built with volunteer labor from the community. In 1896, three years after Madera County broke away from Fresno County, the county built a floating bridge across the South Fork. The following year the San Joaquin Light and Power Company, builders of the dam at Bass Lake, erected a generator in a small stone building alongside the creek, and supplied North Fork with electricity.

When Sierra National Forest was established in 1905, the first Forest Supervisor Walter Shinn had his office in his North Fork home. Named by his wife Julia for the quiet peace and tranquility of its surroundings, the "Peace Cabin" still stands on property now owned by Madera County.

Early North Fork Ranger Stations

The first Forest Supervisor of Sierra National Forest
lived and worked out of his home from 1902-1906.
(Charles Reed Collection photo, courtesy of Mildred Reed)

The second Ranger Station was owned by the government.
It was used from 1906 to 1911.
(John Hawksworth Collection, Fresno Flats Historical Park)

The Associated Lumber and Box Company bought 135 acres between the North and South Forks of Willow Creek in 1941, and began erecting a sawmill to process timber from the nearby forest, primarily for the company-owned box factory in Fresno that supplied wooden boxes for San Joaquin Valley agricultural needs. Powered by steam from two sawdust-burning boilers, the sawmill cut its first lumber in 1943, and the economy of North Fork thrived. In the post World War II years of the late 1940s, the community boasted of having gas stations, several restaurants and inns, four grocery stores, a pharmacy, a hardware store, a movie theatre, and a school with more than 200 students. The times were good in North Fork, and getting better as more and more trees were felled in the forest. While the mill changed hands several times, steady employment continued. In the 1960s, the USFS was turning out timber sales as fast as they could, and by 1968 the mill's annual payroll exceeded $1.25 million.

The growing environmental movement of the 1970s and 80s questioned the Forest Service's annual allowable cut, and effectively had thousands of acres made "Off Limits" by pressuring Congress to establish *Wilderness Areas*. None of these affected the North Fork area, however, and locally the expansion of new roads into previously uncut timber continued. In spite of the creation of the Kaiser Peak Wilderness Area in 1976 and the Dinkey Lakes Wilderness Area in 1984, timber production in Sierra National Forest reached a peak of about 143,000,000 board feet annually for the years 1985 to 1990. That is enough to build 12,000 new homes each year.

Finally environmental pressures on the Forest Service began to take their toll. As old timber sales contracts were fulfilled, new timber sales were delayed or dropped completely as the USFS significantly cut back on timber production. The early 1990s saw fewer and fewer log-laden trucks heading to the few remaining sawmills in North Fork, Auberry and Dinuba. North Fork and its sawmill began to fall on hard times. Inevitably layoffs began, and the economy of North Fork began to suffer. The final blow came on February 25, 1994, when the North Fork mill cut its last log. Ultimately, 45 people lost their timber-industry jobs forever, and the sawmill equipment was sold off at auction. Attempts were made to revive the shattered local economy by the construction of a co-generation plant at the old mill site in mid-1990s, but that did not last either.

The spirit of the mill is preserved today in the traditional Fourth of July Loggers' Jamboree sponsored by the North Fork Boosters. Supporting the North Fork Recreation Center, the annual event features a pancake breakfast, barbeque, dance, and a myriad of logging events and contests.

North Fork's Glory Days of 1948

North Fork still had a tree growing in the middle of Main Street.

The North Fork Garage still utilized hand-pumped,
gravity feed gasoline dispensers.
(photos from Charles Reed Collection, courtesy of Mildred Reed)

The Corral Café, where North Fork's elite went to eat.
(John Hawksworth Collection, Fresno Flats Historical Park)

While North Fork has no motels, there are bed and breakfast establishments to provide overnight accommodations. Breakfast, lunch, and dinner can be obtained in any of the several local eateries. Cold drinks, pre-packaged sandwiches and snacks are available at the market and also at the local convenience stores. Motorists should check their fuel tanks before leaving town, because it could be nearly 100 miles before you see another gas pump.

Also recommended is a visit to the Sierra National Forest North Fork Ranger Station, in order to obtain up to date information about road conditions along the Sierra Vista National Scenic Byway. If you plan to camp or otherwise build a campfire, be sure to pick up a campfire permit. They are necessary, and issued at no cost. The Ranger Station is just off the north end of Main Street at 57003 Road 225 and is open 8 a.m. to 4:30 p.m. Monday through Friday. While you are there, be sure to take the ¼-mile long Cedars Interpretive Trail, an easy, wheel chair accessible nature trail along the North Fork of Willow Creek. Signs along the trail will describe the local flora, fauna, and cultural history of the area.

Motoring into the countryside has long been a favorite pastime.

Sierra Vista National Scenic Byway
Part 2

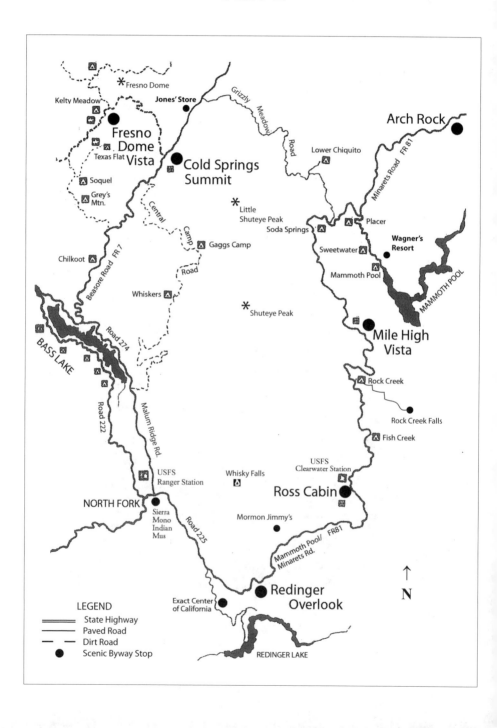

Part 2

North Fork To Grizzly Meadow Road

36.4 miles of paved highway, the first 20 miles of which are open most of the year

In this first section of the Sierra Vista National Scenic Byway, we will climb up through the lower oak woodland of the Sierra Nevada foothills into the mixed forest of oaks, pines, cedars, and firs. We will have the opportunity to make side trips to such places as the exact center of California and Mammoth Pool Reservoir, with its impressive earth-filled dam. We can stop and visit the historic cabin built by pioneer Jesse Ross in the late 1860s, and we can take a short side trip to Mormon Jimmy's cabin, hand crafted in the 1890s, and hear the tragic story of his life. We will learn about John French's trail of 1879-80 to Mammoth City and of modern day efforts to reestablish the historic trail. Finally, we will experience breathtaking views of the Sierra Nevada Crest from Mile High Vista.

0.0   We start our adventure on the Sierra Vista National Scenic Byway in downtown North Fork at the Crazy Y, the intersection where the north end of the main street intersects with Roads 222 and 225 near the post office, market, and the driveway leading to the Bass Lake District Ranger Station of Sierra National Forest. Locals call this intersection the "Crazy Y," because of the odd angle at which the roads join, and the fact that large trucks sometimes become hung up while trying to turn onto Road 222 (Manzanita Road).

The Crazy Y intersection of North Fork

If you need any drinks, snacks, sandwiches, or ice for the cooler, they can all be obtained at the market and several mini-marts here in North Fork. Now is the time to stock up, because those items are in short supply where you are going. Before you leave town, be sure to top off your fuel tank as well, and check with the ranger station for current road conditions.

Reset your trip odometer to zero here at the Crazy Y, and head east out of town on Road 225. Almost immediately the road crosses the North Fork of Willow Creek.

0.2   (0.2) Road 274 (Malum Ridge Road) comes downhill from the left to end at this intersection with Road 225. Road 228 begins here to the right. We will want to go straight ahead on Road 225; however, if you look up to the right, on the embankment overlooking the S.E. corner you will see the Sierra Mono Indian Museum. Various exhibits, including an excellent Indian basket, beadwork, and cradleboard collection, as well as well-known wildlife exhibit, portray the Native American way of life as it has existed in this corner of the Sierra Nevada. Call (559) 877-2115 for the hours of opening of this worthwhile stop.

The Sierra Mono Indian Museum

0.5   (0.3) A short distance beyond, Road 230 to the left leads to the North Fork Recreation Center, where the annual Loggers Jamboree is held over the first weekend in July. Just beyond, Road 225 crosses the bridge over the South Fork of Willow Creek.

0.8   (0.3) In the cleared area to the left was once the log yard for the sawmill, the economic heart of North Fork from 1943 to 1994. Many of the mill workers lived in the wooden houses on the south side of the road. There are plans to develop the old mill site into other commercial uses as soon as the diesel contamination issues are resolved.

Associated Lumber & Box Company mill in 1948
(Gary L. Williams Collection, Fresno Flats Historical Park)

The North Fork's sawmill in 1983 when operated by
American Forest Products
(John Hawksworth Collection, Fresno Flats Historical Park)

1.2   (0.4) Road 223 on the left, heads up the hill to the east to the Cascadel Woods subdivision. This is also the way to pretty little Whisky Falls, via Forest Roads 8S09 and 8S70.

    Road 225 now begins its very gradual climb into the high country. You may notice the strange street names appearing on the right. This area is part of the North Fork Rancheria, where the names were given by the Western Monos living here.

Western Wallflower

Should you pass this way in the springtime, you are likely to find Western wallflower *Erysimum capitatum* growing along the roadside here. A member of the mustard family, it can easily be recognized by its erect stalk, standing up to 2½ feet tall and topped with a bright orange flower cluster. Blooming from March to July, this is one of those wildflowers whose habitat extends from the dry foothills all the way up into the Lodgepole pine-Red fir forest.

2.5   (1.3) Watch for a USFS sign on the right that indicates the current status of the Sierra Vista National Scenic Byway. This information is most important in the wintertime, when a portion of the byway is closed by snow. It will let you know how far up the byway it should be safe to travel.

4.3   (1.8) [Elevation 2,600'] Road 225, also known as the Italian Bar Road, goes off to the right to cross the San Joaquin River above Redinger Lake. If you wish to take Optional Side Trip #1 (see pages 96-97) to the Exact Center of California Monument, turn to the right here. The Sierra Vista National Scenic Byway continues straight ahead on Forest Road 81, now called the Minarets Road.

4.7   (0.4) Soon after crossing Indian Creek, a sign on the right indicates this is a National Forest Scenic Byway. The designation was made on July 14, 1989, as a component of Sierra National Forest's overall recreation plan.

Interior live oak is the predominate vegetation
along the lower byway.

Continue on up the byway, passing hillsides covered with live oak and Digger pine. While many oaks are deciduous, dropping their leaves each fall, live oaks are evergreens. There are two species of live oak in the Sierra Nevada, the Canyon live oak *Quercus chrysolepis* and the Interior live oak *Q. wislizenii*. It is the latter that is most common here. Their dense dark green foliage provides protected roosting places for many birds.

Another common shrub of the foothill chaparral seen along the roadsides for the next ten miles is the manzanita of the genus *Arctostaphylos*. This shrub can be easily recognized by its very smooth reddish brown bark, its clusters of pinkish blossoms in the spring, that turn to green, then red berries in the summer. There are 57 species of manzanita in California, of which eight are found in the Sierra Nevada. The species most common here is the Greenleaf manzanita *A. patula*. The name *manzanita* comes from the Spanish word meaning "little apple," but the berry is far too bitter to eat raw. Native Americans would crush the fruit, then put the mash into a basket, where it was leeched with copious amounts of hot water to remove the bitter tannic acid. The resulting meal was then hand formed into patties, and baked on hot rocks. The local Miwok Indians also brewed a berry cider that was a refreshing drink at summer gatherings.

Manzanita blossoms and berries

The predominate conifer tree in this lower part of Sierra National Forest is the tall and often leaning Digger or bull pine *Pinus sabiniana*. Although pines generally rank as an important source of timber, the USFS has little interest in harvesting this resource. Its course-grained wood tends to warp badly when dried, and thus it is not thought of as a timber tree. Digger pines are sometimes cut up and used for firewood, but, even then, they are not favored since the wood burns fast and is full of pitch that tends to leave a creosote residue in chimneys and fireplace flues. That is not to say that the Digger pine is useless, however. The tree produces large heavy cones with inch-long spines or hooks. The cones contain nutritious nuts (they are high

40

in proteins and fat) that were relished by Native Americans and, together with acorns, were a staple part of the Indian diet. Squirrels, woodpeckers and jays also utilize the nuts of the Digger pine.

Should you pass this way early on a mid-summer morning, you may notice the low sun highlighting the many spider webs along the embankment on the left side of the roadway as it skirts around the base of Castle Peak [Elevation 4082']. These were made by the Funnel web spider of the family *Agelenidae*. These little critters spin a

Digger Pine

silky web around their burrow. When an insect lands on the sticky web, the spider senses the vibrations and rushes out to bite the insect, before carrying it down the funnel into its den. The bite of one species living in Australia is deadly to humans; however, those living here are harmless.

The homes of the Funnel web spider are commonly seen along the lower byway during the summer months.

6.3 (1.6) A sign on the right indicates you are now entering Sierra National Forest. For the next 30 miles, the scenic byway will also carry the designation of Forest Road 81.

America's "National Forests" go back to 1891, when President Benjamin Harrison signed legislation that enabled the eventual creation of a forest reserve system in 1893. Originally there were six forest reserves nationwide, of which the Sierra Forest Reserve was the largest. Government agents slowly began to get a handle on uncontrolled logging and grazing, but it soon became obvious that the Forest Reserves would have to be broken up into more manageable size units. In 1905 the U.S. Forest Service was established, and with it the six million acre Sierra National Forest. But even then the size of the forest proved to be unwieldy, so it was ultimately broken up into a half-dozen more national forest units. Today, Sierra National Forest covers some 1.3 million acres, which are subdivided into two Ranger Districts. Overall responsibility rests with the Forest Supervisor whose office is in Clovis CA. Reporting to the Supervisor are two District Rangers whose offices are in North Fork and Prather.

6.8   (0.5) **Stop #1: Redinger Overlook** [Elevation 3320']

From the small parking area on the right, you can look south down into the San Joaquin River Canyon to see Redinger Lake, formed by the third highest dam on the main San Joaquin River. The two upper dams at Mammoth Pool and Redinger were built by the Southern California Edison Company to hold water for hydroelectric generating plants. Completed in 1951, this reservoir was named for David H. Redinger, resident engineer of SCE's Big Creek Hydroelectric Project for thirty years.

Boating and water skiing are the most popular activities on the three-mile-long lake, as fishing from its waters is not the best. Lying at an elevation of 1,400 feet, the waters of the lake seem to be a little cool for warm water fish such as bass, and not cold enough for cold water fish like trout. (The Redinger Lake boat ramp can be accessed from county Roads 225 and 235.)

One of the powerhouses along the San Joaquin River
(Gary L. Williams photo)

42

This is the land of the Blue oak *Quercus douglasii* that, together with the Digger pine *Pinus sabiniana*, is the most common tree in the lower western foothills of the Sierra Nevada. The bluish tinge of the leaves is from a waxy coating that helps reduce moisture loss during the heat of summer. The Blue oak also shares its foothill habitat with two cousins: the Valley oak *Quercus lobata* and the Black oak *Quercus kelloggii*. The generous crop of acorns provided by these trees each fall was a staple food of Native Americans, who pounded them into a meal and leeched the resulting flour with hot water to remove the excess tannin, before fashioning the gruel into patties that were baked. Acorns are also a favorite food of many birds, deer, and other animals that inhabit this foothill belt.

The Blue oak in the winter without its leaves

You may notice a dense green growth on the branches of some of the oaks. This is particularly noticeable in the winter when the tree has shed its leaves. What you are seeing is Oak mistletoe *Phoradendron villosum*, a parasite. Most plants utilize chlorophyll to manufacture their own food. Parasites lack this substance, and they obtain their food by stealing it from a host. Mistletoe is such a parasite. It sinks its roots into the cambium layer beneath the oak's bark to tap into the moisture, nutrients, and minerals being utilized by the tree. In the winter when the oak has dropped its leaves, the mistletoe stands out in dense clusters on the otherwise bare branches of the oak. There is a different type of mistletoe for each type of tree. Thus, it is the *P. libocedri* that grows on the incense cedar, *P. juniperinum* on the Sierra juniper, and *Arceuthobium campylopodum* that attaches itself to pines and firs. In theory, these infestations could become so severe that the host is sucked dry and killed, but that rarely seems to happen in trees.

Mistletoe on an oak tree

Do not mistake the growth of mistletoe on oaks for that of a burl. A burl is an aberrant growth similar to cancer in a human, except the burl does not kill the tree. In redwood trees the burl can actually develop sprouts and grow after the tree itself dies. However, that is not the case with oaks.

This enormous oak burl can be seen along
Forest Road 8S27 to Mormon Jimmy's.

As you leave the Redinger Overlook, you may get a glimpse of Musick Mountain, seven miles away and almost due east across the canyon of the San Joaquin River. The mountain has a still useable, but seldom staffed fire lookout tower on its 6,801 summit. Continue on up the scenic byway.

8.7   (1.9) As you come around this curve, the high point of mostly bare granite on the right is 6,194' Source Point.

10.2   (1.5) The road crosses Saginaw Creek, a small stream that begins on the south face of Whiskey Ridge and flows down into Redinger Lake.

10.4   (0.2) [Elevation 4,160'] Forest Road 8S27 on the left goes less than a mile to the site of Mormon Jimmy's cabin and mine, and ultimately beyond to the Cascadel Woods subdivision. The gate on this road is closed from December 1st to May 1st of each year, ostensibly to protect wildlife habitat. Nevertheless, even during the winter months the scenic byway is usually snow-free to this point and, should you find the gate locked, the easy walk of about a mile to Mormon Jimmy's cabin can make for a pleasant outing in December and January, when the San Joaquin Valley is shrouded in fog and gloom. If you wish to take Optional Side Trip #2 (see pages 98-99) to Mormon Jimmy's cabin and mine, turn left (or park safely off the road) here.

13.4   (3.0) The road to the right goes down to Kinsman Flat, a section of privately owned land. The first white man to settle in this area is said to have been Joe Kinsman who arrived around 1851. Not finding any gold, he settled down and eventually married an Indian woman. It was he who named Hooker's Creek and Hooker's Cove after "Fighting Joe Hooker," a Major General in the Union Army, and a man he so admired.

The story is told of how Kinsman would feed his pigs acorns all summer to fatten them. When it came time to sell them in the fall, he would put a sack of grain in the back of his wagon and punch a small hole in it, allowing the grain to dribble out very slowly. The pigs happily followed the wagon all the way to Stockton!

It was also in this area that in July of 1939 the destructive Source Point Fire broke out, apparently caused by a negligent fisherman. It jumped over the San Joaquin River into Fresno County, and threatened to burn all the way to Huntington Lake. At night the glow from the fire could be seen in Fresno. More than 1,000 firefighters worked to contain it, an incredible number in those days. **Remember: be very careful with fire here in the forest!**

13.9 (0.5) Forest Road 8S03 on the right goes nearly four miles down into the canyon to the Mammoth Pool Powerhouse on the San Joaquin River. It is here that the water coming out of the eight-mile long tunnel and penstock below Mammoth Pool Reservoir is turned into electricity, after which the water is returned to the river. Anglers can access the San Joaquin River, although a locked gate prevents motor vehicles from crossing the bridge beyond the powerhouse.

Southern California Edison Company's
Mammoth Pool Powerhouse

14.1 (0.2) From a gravel turnout on the right side of the byway, there is a nice view down into the bottom of the San Joaquin River Canyon. The high mountain on the other side of the canyon is the western end of Kaiser Ridge. The bare outcrops of granitic rock were rounded not by glaciers, but by a geologic phenomenon called *exfoliation*. It is a process where the outer layers of crystalline igneous rocks peel off like an onionskin. Glaciers can also grind granite smooth, but in this case, the lowest point of the San Joaquin Glacier terminated about seven miles up the canyon.

Exfoliation of granodiorite on Shuteye Peak

15.3   (1.2) **Stop #2: Jesse Ross Cabin** [Elevation 4,000']

Turn left off the byway onto Forest Road 4S81K and into a small parking area with a restroom. From the parking area, it is an easy walk of about 100 yards on a trail to the cabin.

Prospector Jesse Blakely Ross built this cabin of rough-hewn Ponderosa pine logs in the late 1860s. Located just below the snow level at 4,000 feet at what was then the 'end of the road,' it is one of the oldest structures in Madera County. When Jesse built the cabin, he was a bachelor and he thought it was plenty big for his modest needs. A few years later, he met and married Mary Waspi, a local Mono Indian. In December of 1871, Mary gave birth to a little girl who they named Julia Belle Ross. Some years later the ground floor of the cabin was partitioned off and, for a short time, stairs went to the second floor.

Ross planted a five-acre apple orchard near the cabin, originally built on a parcel of land about ½ mile on up the road. He also planted wheat and pink beans on the ranch, and harvested them for sale in Fresno. Jesse posthumously received a Homestead Patent from the U.S. Government in 1900, shortly after he had died and been buried near Ross Creek. The land passed through the hands of Julia, who died in 1904, and her husband George Hallock, before being purchased by Samuel L. Hogue in 1910.

Hogue had been the first schoolteacher in Selma and also served as a Justice of the Peace in Fresno. He moved his family into the log house that Jesse Ross had built, and renamed it the "Hogue Ranch." He planted more apple trees and beans to satisfy the demand for the fruits and vegetables that helped to prevent "land scurvy." Just as sailors got sick, so scurvy weakened the early miners, timber jacks and cattlemen, and they fell prey to the elements and exposure. There was plenty of game and fish, but they needed fruit and vegetables to remain healthy. Hogue and his sons even built a small sawmill with a wooden waterwheel on Ross Creek in order to make apple boxes for shipping the fruit, and continued to raise pink beans as well as hogs until he sold his ranch in 1930. The Hogue Ranch has passed through several more owners since that time.

In 1990, the cabin was given to the U.S. Forest Service by Richard and Jeanetta McClurg, with the provision that it be moved off the private property and preserved. Thanks to the dedication and hard work of dozens of citizen-volunteers who dismantled the fireplace stone by stone, a house moving company was able to jack up the cabin, place rubber-tired dollies underneath, and move it in one piece without damage to its present location near the Clearwater Station, where the fireplace and chimney were reassembled. Participants in a class offered by the USFS in 1991 learned the art of restoration, and any logs needing replacement were hand hewn, using tools of the 1860s. Now in a similar environmental setting as the original location, the cabin has been completed and opened to the public for viewing. Be sure to check out the newspapers from 1893 to 1945 that were used as wallpaper. Enjoy this historic treasure of the past, but leave it as you find it for others to enjoy. **Remember: it is a violation of Federal law to destroy or remove artifacts from historical sites.**

The Ross Cabin

The Ross cabin at the Hogue Ranch, circa 1955
(Bud Miller Collection, Fresno Flats Historical Park)

The Ross Cabin today

On the walk back to the parking area, take a look at the one to two-foot high groundcover with tiny fern-like leaves. Break off a small piece, and rub it vigorously in your palms. Do you detect a pungent odor? The plant is *Chamaebatia foliolosa* most commonly called by its Miwok Indian name, kitkitdizze; it is also called Bear clover, Tarweed, or Mountain Misery. The Miwoks and other Indian peoples would steep its leaves in hot water, and drink the resulting tea as a medicine for a variety of ailments. There is an old myth, perhaps first told by early mountain men and fur trappers, that bears would roll in the carpet-like plant so that the resinous sticky substance on the leaves would adhere to their fur, and thus ward off mosquitoes.

The tiny fern-like leaves of the Kitkitdizze
produce a pungent odor when crushed.

15.5 (0.2) Leave the Ross Cabin parking lot, and make a left turn back onto the byway. On the east side of the byway, across from the parking area, a trail sign points to the east. This hiking trail soon connects with the French Trail (26E16), where a left turn will eventually take you up the canyon into the Ansel Adams Wilderness and to the Squaw Dome Trailhead. A right turn will take you down to Hookers Creek below Kinsman Flat. From there, it is possible to hike on down to the San Joaquin River at Italian Bar. Today the French Trail is used mainly by fishermen and backpackers, but it once was a vital trans-Sierra pack trail and, before that, an old Indian trade route.

The French Trail

The French Trail is a route between the western foothills of the San Joaquin Valley and Mammoth Lakes on the east side of the Sierra Nevada. Over the years there has been a lot of confusion about its route. The reader should understand, however, that there are three different variations of the "French Trail."

It all started when a civil engineer by the name of John S. French recognized the great need for the several thousand residents of the Lake Mining District and the booming mining camp of Mammoth City to be readily connected with the San Joaquin Valley, just fifty miles to the west. French scouted the mountainous terrain, and built his first horse trail in the late spring and early summer of 1879. He advertised a $29.00 fare from San Francisco to Mammoth City, of which the first $14.00 was on existing public transportation by train and stagecoach to Madera and Fresno Flats (present day Oakhurst). For the remaining $15.00, the traveler would get on a horse owned by French and be led by French himself, north via the wagon road to the Madera Flume & Trading Company's sawmill at Gooseberry Flat. From there French's original trail went to Beasore Meadows, where overnight lodging was provided in a cabin he had built, with meals prepared by a Chinese cook hired by French. Leaving early the next day, the traveler would be taken through Jackass Meadows and down to the Sheep Crossing of the North Fork of the San Joaquin River (so named because while grazing cattle would swim across the river, sheep required a primitive bridge be built to cross it), on up above the Middle Fork to Lion Point, then down to Red's Meadow and on into Mammoth City, a total of 35 miles in twelve hours. We do not know how many paying passengers French had that summer.

The next spring, he started his second version of the French Trail. This one would be clear of snow for a few more months of the year and, hopefully, could be converted to a wagon road. French's second trail, the *river route*, used existing wagon roads from Millerton to Brown's Place (present day North Fork) and on to the Jesse Ross cabin (later known as the Hogue Apple Ranch). From there he built a pack trail up the west side of the San Joaquin River Canyon, trying to stay about 1,000 feet above the river and below the snow line.

Unfortunately, the mines of Mammoth City failed to produce the wealth predicted, and by 1881 the camp had gone bust. There was no longer much need for a trans-Sierra pack trail, much less a wagon road. Nevertheless, Jesse Ross and his brother Cal still occasionally used the trail into the 1890s to pack supplies in for prospectors. In the 125 years since French built his *river route*, the trail has been overgrown with brush and pretty much obliterated. In the summer of 1910, Forest Ranger Audie Wofford spent a lot of time trying to retrace the thirty-year-old trail. Even then, French's route was badly overgrown and difficult to find and follow. In many places Wofford had only blaze marks cut into trees to guide him.

Old blaze in oak tree   Tool cache found along lower French Trail

And this brings us to the third French Trail, the modern day version built by the USFS along the approximate route of French's 1880 river route. Today's hiking trail (USFS Trail 26E16) starts on the east side of the byway, across from the present day Ross Cabin parking area. It will take you north to Wagner's Store on the Mammoth Pool Road and beyond, where it crosses the trail down to Hell's Half Acre just inside the Ansel Adams Wilderness. Eventually, it will take you back to the scenic byway at either the South Fork or the McCreary trailhead. Today's hiking trail does not make the dangerous crossing of lower Granite Creek.

If you wish to get a taste of the sights that French saw along his trail, and if you can arrange a car shuttle, we suggest that you leave a car at Wagner's Store and Resort [Elevation 3,700'], then drive on up to either the Hell's Half Acre [Elevation 6,000'] or South Fork [Elevation 6,400'] trailhead. The hike back to Wagner's Resort can be done in a day. The procedure would be the same for those wishing to backpack, except we suggest you start at the McCreary Meadow trailhead [Elevation 6,800'], hiking as far as Jackass Creek the first day, and easily finishing the fifteen-mile hike on the second day.

It might also be noted that the San Joaquin River Council, a coalition of private organizations, is advocating the rebuilding of parts of the old French Trail to incorporate them into a modern day San Joaquin River Trail, which will connect the 73 miles between Millerton Lake and the Pacific Crest Trail near the Devil's Postpile National Monument. This group is doing much more than simply promoting the idea. They are actively working with principal land managers along the route, the California State Parks Department, the U.S. Bureau of Land Management, and the U.S. Forest Service, to make this vision a reality. They also have periodic weekend work parties to do actual trail and bridge construction. So far, about 40 miles of the 73 total miles are completed. You might take a look at their website: www.sanjoaquinrivertrailcouncil.org for more information.

15.7 (0.2) The USFS Clearwater Station is on the left. During the summer months the USFS has a wildland fire engine with a crew of five on duty here, one of seven such engines strategically placed throughout Sierra National Forest. While Clearwater Station is "home" to Engine 52, it is considered a firefighting resource and, as such, the apparatus and the personnel assigned to it could be sent to a fire anywhere in the Western United States on a few minutes notice.

15.8 (0.1) The byway crosses Clearwater Creek, whose headwaters are on the eastern flank of Source Peak.

16.2 (0.4) Here is the parcel of private land known by locals as the "Hogue Ranch" or, in more recent years, the "Apple Ranch". This is the area where Jesse Ross built his cabin in the late 1860s. RV sales mogul Dan Gamel currently owns the land, and an RV park may be in its future.

16.5 (0.3) [Elevation 4,320'] The byway now crosses Ross Creek, the original site of Ross Cabin. Jesse and Julia are buried somewhere nearby along its bank. A hiking trail on the left descends a little to connect with the French Trail mentioned back at the 15.5-mile point.

18.1 (1.6) The once oiled (not recommended for standard passenger automobiles) Forest Road 7S07 to the left goes 13 miles to Whisky Falls and back down the other side to South Fork. This road, too, is closed from December 1st to May 1st to prevent ruts and soil erosion.

18.7 (0.6) [Elevation 4,600'] The USFS Fish Creek Campground is on the right. While this small seven-unit campground has no spaces suitable for trailers, it is nevertheless popular with tent campers. Tables, fireplaces and a vault toilet are provided, although water is not. On a first come - first served basis, there is no campground host, but a modest fee to camp here is charged during the summer months. Fish Creek runs through the campground to the delight of children. The California Department of Fish and Game stocks the stream with pan-size trout, a fact that delights anglers.

19.1 (0.4) Access to the modern day French Trail can be made on right.

20.9 (1.8) Ahead, high above the highway, we now get our first good view up towards 8,351' Shuteye Peak. Although it cannot be seen from this vantage point, Shuteye Peak has a fire lookout structure on its summit. It is one of the few fire lookouts on the Sierra National Forest still staffed during the summer and early fall months.

The high peaks on the western slopes of the Sierra Nevada were used as observation posts for fire detection as early as 1900. The first two lookout structures were built in 1908, not too long after the system of national forests was established. During the 1930s, the Civilian Conservation Corps (CCC) built, and rebuilt, over 200 similar facilities. Eventually six hundred of these sites would be established. The times have changed, however. With Federal budgetary limitations, most fire lookouts have been closed. By

1986, California only had 185 lookouts still open, and today the number is even less.

The Shuteye Peak fire lookout

Recognizing that the foundation of fire control was early detection, rangers had been using a rocky pillar near the Peace Cabin known as "Sight Rock" to spot telltale plumes of smoke on the horizon (other forests often used a "lookout tree"). Forest Service records are not too clear about when the first fire lookout was stationed on top of Shuteye Peak. One document suggests 1905, the same year that the Sierra National Forest was established. Before his death, Audie Wofford, who claimed to be the first lookout and was known for his "Get them early when they're small" byword, says that in 1907 he and a man named Weltie camped in Brown's Meadow at the southwest base of the mountain, and made the 1,500-foot climb every day between July 5th and September 15th. They spotted four fires that season. As a result, Audie said a trail to the summit was built in 1908, and the first lookout structure was built in 1909. The lookout has been replaced twice since then: once in 1915 after heavy snow caused the original one to collapse, and once in 1957.

A Century of Fire Suppression on Sierra National Forest

The first lookout structure on Shuteye Peak was built around 1909, and destroyed by snow in the winter of 1914-15.

The second Shuteye fire lookout circa 1915
(Charles Reed Collection, courtesy Mildred Reed)

Early forest firefighters even rode the rails at times.
(Madera County Historical Society photo)

22.1 (1.2) The byway now crosses Slide Creek, a small watercourse which originates just below Cold Springs Meadow. Slide Creek flows into Rock Creek just below the byway.

22.4 (0.3) The entrance to the popular Rock Creek Campground [Elevation 4,300'] is on the right. It is here that, for three days each October, Native Americans hold a bear dance to put the bears to sleep. They return each April for the dance to wake the sleeping bears. Of the six USFS campgrounds directly on the Sierra Vista National Scenic Byway, this is the lowest in elevation, and thus puts the campground below the snow line for nine or ten months of the year. The presence of Rock Creek makes this one of the more popular along the entire 90-mile route. It has nineteen camping units, of which thirteen are suitable for trailers. Tables, fireplaces, drinking water, and a vault toilet are provided. There is a campground host, and a modest fee is charged to camp here during the summer months.

Just inside the campground entrance, the once-oiled Forest Road 7S47 drops steeply for 1,250 feet into the San Joaquin River gorge to Rock Creek Falls. **That road is only recommended for vehicles having high clearance and four-wheel drive.** The route is described in Optional Side Trip #3 on pages 100-101.

23.3 (0.9) Forest Road 7S02 goes off to the left. It climbs to Brown's Meadow (9 miles) and eventually goes on to the fourteen-unit Whisky Falls Campground (14 miles). The route is well marked. The USFS closes and locks the gate on this road during the winter months.

23.4 (0.1) The byway now crosses the Rock Creek bridge [Elevation 4,550']. The pools and smooth rocks just downstream from the bridge make a favorite place for kids to play in summer.

For those who are geologically aware, you may soon notice a change in the bedrock geology. For the past many miles, the byway had been passing through an igneous rock called granodiorite. It is a close relative of granite, except it has a little less plagioclase feldspar and a little more of other minerals. Technically, granodiorite is probably more common in the Sierra Nevada than is granite. This igneous rock was part of the Sierra Nevada batholith that rose to the surface from great depths during the first half of the Cretaceous Period about 100-120 million years ago. When the batholith was pushed up through the preexisting layers of older marine sediments, they were transformed by heat and pressure from sedimentary rocks into metamorphic rocks. Over the last 100 million years, most of those pre-batholith rocks have been eroded away, as the Sierra Nevada Range rose up even higher than it is today. However, there are still a few places where these old sediments, now turned into metamorphic rocks, still can be seen. The byway goes through such an area for the next couple of miles.

Geologists call these isolated pockets of pre-existing rocks roof pendants. In the limited areas in the Sierra Nevada where roof pendants exist, it is not uncommon to find the minerals containing tungsten, molybdenum, and vanadium.

Very old metamorphic rocks are exposed in several
road cuts along this portion of the byway.

25.0 (1.6) The site of the Wissman Mine is on the right. These tungsten claims were located in December of 1940 by Charles Wissman. During this period, France had already fallen to Nazi Germany, and England was fighting for its life. American involvement in the war in Europe was only a matter of time, and tungsten was already in great demand to harden steel. Wissman erected a concentrating mill in 1942, and shipped out small amounts of tungsten concentrates. Production was small, and there is little to see today. John French's second trans-Sierra trail passed through this same area in 1880.

26.6 (1.6) [Elevation 5,393'] This spot is known as Mile High Curve. In the early 1960s, shortly after the road was built for the construction of the Mammoth Pool Dam, this curve in the road became a favorite stopping place for passing motorists, because of the expansive and grand views it offers to the east onto the High Sierra skyline. Stop if you wish, but the view is just as nice a half-mile ahead, where there is more parking.

27.2 (0.6) **Stop #3: Mile High Vista** [Elevation 5,400']

Turn to the right here to see Mile High Vista, one of the highlights of the Sierra Vista National Scenic Byway. Next to the parking area, there are two picnic tables and two vault toilets making this viewpoint a great picnic area. A diorama points out the various topographic features on the spectacular skyline of the Sierra Crest to the east, including the Minarets,

13,157' Mount Ritter, and Mammoth Mountain, and at least fifteen other named peaks over 10,000 feet high. The highest and steepest mountain range in the continental United States, its name Sierra Nevada means Snowy Mountain Range in Spanish. The incredible expanse of the Ansel Adams, Kaiser, and John Muir Wilderness Areas also lies before you.

There are particularly fine views down into the gorge of the Middle Fork of the San Joaquin River below. During the seven glacial advances and subsequent retreats of the Sierra Nevada ice sheets in the two million year long Pleistocene Ice Age, great rivers of ice were slowly pushed down all of the major west-facing canyons in the Sierra Nevada. At its peak, the glacier in the San Joaquin River canyon was well over thirty-miles long, perhaps second only to the Tuolumne glacier that was sixty-miles long, and extended down to 2,000 feet. At one time, the tip of the San Joaquin Glacier extended down to around 3,200 feet, about the same location as the Mammoth Pool Dam today. In the process, the slow moving ice ground away the igneous rock in its path. When the last of this great ice melted some 12,000 years ago, such ice-rounded features as Balloon Dome and Squaw Dome were left on either side of the gorge. These are two of the several domes to be seen by looking up the river.

Fuller Buttes (left) and Balloon Dome (right)
as seen up the canyon

Left to right: 10,562' Sing Peak, 10,509' Madera Peak, and The Balls

Eagle Beak Peak towers above Mile High Vista

27.5 (0.3) Upon leaving Mile High Vista, turn right back onto the byway. About a mile up the road, you will leave the previously mentioned roof pendant of old metamorphic bedrock, and return to the familiar granodiorite.

29.9 (2.4) The scenic byway crosses Shakeflat Creek, a minor tributary to the San Joaquin River.

31.4 (1.5) On the left is the trailhead for a strenuous and little-used hiking trail that climbs some 2,100' to Shuteye Pass, where another climb of 1000' will bring you to the fire lookout on the summit of 8,351' Shuteye Peak.

There is also a rough jeep trail to the top of Shuteye Peak from the western side of the mountain. If you have a four-wheel drive vehicle and would like to take this scenic route some day, see *High Sierra SUV Trails Volume II – the Western Slope* for a description of the route.

31.7 (0.3) The byway now crosses Shuteye Creek, a tributary to the larger Chiquito Creek to the north.

32.6 (0.9) High and to the left in this area there are some nice views of 8,351' Shuteye Peak.

33.4 (0.8) The byway crosses Dutch Oven Creek.

35.0 (1.6) The byway crosses the west fork of Chiquito Creek.

35.4 (0.4) [Elevation 4,300'] The USFS Soda Springs Campground is on the right. There are sixteen camping spaces, of which seven are suitable for trailers. Tables, fireplaces and a vault toilet are provided, but there is no drinking water.

36.4 (1.0) The junction with the narrow, but paved Forest Road 6S71 (Grizzly Meadow Road) is on the left. If it is becoming late in the day, you may wish to consider ending your byway adventure here today, and returning another day to complete the remaining 54 miles of the Sierra Vista National Scenic Byway. If that is the case, turn left here. After 12 miles, Grizzly Meadow Road comes to Forest Highway 7, and rejoins the byway at the 30.5-mile point in Part 3 of this guide. You will miss some 32 miles of the byway, but also avoid the roughest 10 miles of the entire loop. However, if the day is young and you choose to continue on the scenic byway, stay on Forest Road 81 and continue heading north.

Sierra Vista National Scenic Byway
Part 3

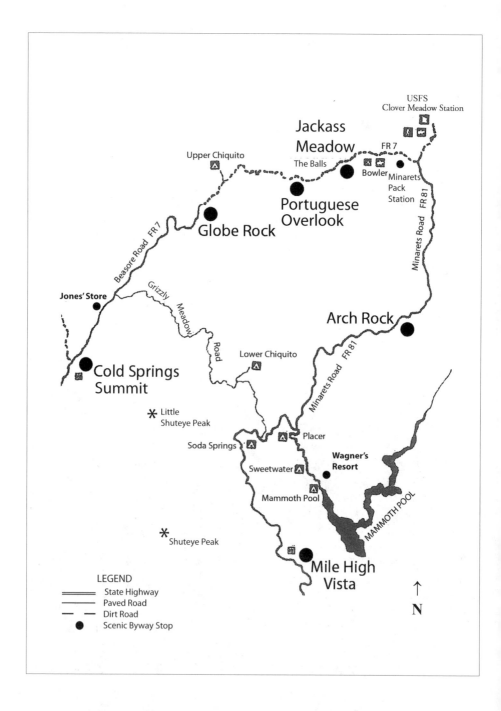

USFS
Clover Meadow Station

Jackass
Meadow

FR 7

Upper Chiquito

The Balls

Bowler Minarets
Pack
Station

Portuguese
Overlook

Minarets Road FR 81

Beasore Road FR 7

Globe Rock

Grizzly

Jones' Store

Meadow

Arch Rock

Road

Lower Chiquito

Minarets Road FR 81

Cold Springs
Summit

✳ Little
Shuteye Peak

Placer

Soda Springs

Wagner's
Resort

Sweetwater

✳ Shuteye Peak

Mammoth Pool

MAMMOTH POOL

Mile High
Vista

LEGEND
State Highway
Paved Road
Dirt Road
● Scenic Byway Stop

↑
N

Part 3

Grizzly Meadow Road
to Cold Springs Summit

Entire route closed by snow from mid November through May, includes 15 miles of high standard highway, 10 miles of graded dirt roadway, then another 8 miles of good highway

In this segment of the Sierra Vista National Scenic Byway, we will have the opportunity to visit Mammoth Pool Reservoir and get a close-up view of its impressive earth-filled dam. We will see such geologic oddities as Arch Rock, columnar basalt, and Globe Rock. We will pass through areas of old Indian summer camps and places where Native Americans from the east and west came to meet and trade various goods. And we will hear tales of the old time packers and cattlemen who came to the high pastures each summer. Finally, off this portion of the byway are opportunities to get out of the car, stretch your legs, and hike to some beautiful high country studded with lakes and watched over by the high Sierra peaks.

0.0   Here is the junction with the narrow, but paved Grizzly Meadow Road (Forest Road 6S71). If you have elected to continue following the byway, stay on Forest Road 81, and proceed north. **Reset your trip odometer to zero** as you begin this segment of the byway.

1.3   (1.3) [Elevation 4,414'] The byway now crosses the Chiquito Creek Bridge. We will cross this same stream again at the 23.5-mile point.

1.9   (0.6) The paved Forest Road 6S25 to the right descends to USFS campgrounds, Wagner's Mammoth Pool Resort, and on to the boat launching ramps on Mammoth Pool Reservoir. Food, fuel, a general store, cabins, a trailer park, and camping are all offered during the summer months. If you wish to take the worthwhile Optional Side Trip #4 down to Mammoth Pool and its dam, turn right here. See pages 102-104.

2.8   (0.9) Nearly a mile beyond the turnoff to Mammoth Pool, the byway comes to Forest Road 6S22 on the right. It goes 1½ miles down to the USFS Little Jackass Campground [Elevation 4,800'], a small five-unit campground suitable for trailers. No potable water is provided, but there are tables and a vault toilet. No fees are charged at this campground.

3.3   (0.5) The USFS Minarets Work Center is on the left. Sierra National Forest personnel use this facility as temporary living quarters and a base of operations during the summer months.

3.4   (0.1) Forest Roads 6S44 and 6S01 go to the left, skirting Arnold Meadow to

Lower Chiquito Campground and beyond, to connect with the paved Grizzly Meadow Road. The USFS Lower Chiquito Campground [Elevation 4,900'] on Chiquito Creek has seven campsites and a vault toilet. There is no piped water, but a fee is charged for camping here.

During the next mile, look ahead and to the north for the rounded top of 7,112' Jackass Rock, which can occasionally be seen through the trees that line the byway. It is difficult to imagine, but a great glacier of ice once covered and wore down this rock during the Pleistocene Ice Age.

5.5   (2.1) The byway crosses the West Fork of Jackass Creek.

7.7   (2.2) The entrance to the privately operated Jackass Rock Organization Camp is passed on the right. It can accommodate several large groups, but reservations must be made through the County of Madera.

8.0   (0.3) The byway crosses Jackass Creek.

8.5   (0.5) The byway now crosses Graveyard Creek that flows south out of Graveyard Meadow. We have heard two explanations as to how the name "Graveyard" was chosen. One is that early sheepherders would camp here summer after summer while grazing their flocks in the high meadows. As the story goes, the shepherds drank a lot around the campfire in the evening. When a whiskey bottle was empty, it was commonly called a "dead soldier." After a few years, there became quite an accumulation of empty bottles scattered about. Hence, a "graveyard" of "dead soldiers." Johnny Jones, a cowboy who spent many summers running cattle in this country, tells another story. He says that late one fall, under threatening skies and snow flurries, he was coming out of McCreary Meadow when he inadvertently rode his horse over what appeared to be two old graves. Because of the threatening weather conditions, he did not stop to investigate the matter, and in subsequent summers he never got back there. Years later, in retelling the story to historian Dwight Barnes, Jones did not recall the location, but thought it might have been Graveyard Meadow.

8.8   (0.3) Forest Road 5S19 on the right goes ¼-mile to the Hells Half Acre trailhead parking area [Elevation 6,200']. Here a hiking trail steeply descends some 2,500 feet to unimproved campsites on the San Joaquin River, where fishing can be quite good. The trail also crosses the French Trail, making possible a pleasant day hike down to Wagner's Resort on the Mammoth Pool Road.

9.3   (0.5) **Stop #4: Arch Rock** [Elevation 6200']

Here on the right, an easy 400-foot long footpath goes down to a viewing platform from which Arch Rock can be seen. Much of the work on this interpretive site was undertaken in 2002 as an Eagle Scout project by Matt Tucker of Troop 1192 in Coarsegold CA.

As you walk down the path to the viewing platform, look for the purple flowers of the Mountain Pride *Penstemon newberryi*, which bloom every summer here on the granitic gravelly slope. The genus *Penstemon* is quite common in California, having 24 different species in just the Sierra Nevada.

The natural arch is a geologic oddity produced by the differential erosion of the granodiorite bedrock. Such features are not commonly found in crystalline igneous rocks. Here, weathering and erosion took place along vertical joints and more horizontal semi-curved exfoliation cracks in the granodiorite. Slight differences in the minerals within the granite-like rock made the upper portion harder than the material a few feet farther down. The forces of moisture, alternately freezing and expanding followed by melting and contracting, gradually broke down the softer minerals. Eventually the harder, more resistant material survived, while the softer underlying material was worn away. The result is Arch Rock.

Arch Rock has been eroded out of the granodiorite bedrock.

9.6 (0.3) Forest Road 5S29 on the right soon leads to Road 5S69, which will take you to the South Fork trailhead [Elevation 6,400']. Here a steep hiking trail descends 1,800 feet to the French Trail, making it possible to go on down to Hell's Half Acre. If you get an early start, it is also possible to hike down to Wagner's Resort in one long day.

10.6 (1.0) Road 5S08 goes to Graveyard Meadow and beyond.

The Brown brothers Herrick and Jerry, descendants of the Wide Awake Ranch family, used Graveyard Meadow as a summer cow camp. In 1916 they built a Ponderosa pine log cabin to use for storage of saddles and food for themselves and their horses, and as a shelter from summer storms. It had no windows, and the only light came from an open door or a lantern. In the fall of 1917 the boys gathered 4800 sugar pine cones to sell to the forest service, which wanted 400 pounds of seeds for a reforesting project. They put a canvas down on the floor, and collected the cones until they had a pile two feet high, thinking that the seeds would fall out as the cones dried during the winter. What a surprise they got when they returned in the spring – small critters had made their way into the cabin and devoured their special stash! The forest service had to go with many fewer seeds for their planned reforestation project that year.

11.9 (1.3) Road 5S65 to the right goes two miles to the Squaw Dome trailhead. From here it is a pleasant vertical climb of about 1,000 feet to the glacially rounded summit of 7,818' Squaw Dome.

13.5 (1.6) The byway crosses Miller Creek for the first time. This same stream will be crossed again near the Minarets Pack Station just a half-mile up the road.

14.8 (1.3) Our scenic byway now reaches a 'T' intersection [Elevation 7,000'] where Forest Road 81 ends and, with it, the high standard asphalt surface also ends. The oiled road 5S30 to the right goes north 1.8 miles to the Clover Meadows Ranger Station (see Optional Side Trip #5 on page 105). To continue following the Sierra Vista National Scenic Byway, turn left.

From the 'T' intersection where Forest Highway 81 ends, the byway now turns west to follow Forest Highway 7, known as Beasore Road, for the next 17 miles. For the next few miles, the road surface is only partially oiled and does not yet have its finish layer of asphalt. This is a top budget priority for the USFS, but money has been tight, and the roadwork has not yet been completed.

Immediately after you make the turn onto Forest Highway 7, a wall of Lodgepole pine hides the view south into Miller Meadow. Native Americans seemed to have camped here and in nearby McCreary and Graveyard Meadows each summer. The area may have been a meeting point where Paiutes from the Mono Lake area would meet with the Yokuts and other peoples from the western foothills of the Sierra Nevada for the purpose of trade. The peoples from the west had acorns to trade. People from the Great Basin had salt, obsidian, and piñon nuts for exchange.

Nearby are several areas where bedrock mortars were used to pound acorns and piñon nuts into a meal with a handheld hammer stone or pestle. The floor of the forest is littered with shiny flakes of dark glass-like obsidian that were left when larger pieces were chipped into arrowheads. There is no local source for this obsidian. It most likely was carried here as trade goods over the Sierra from the Mono Craters area just north of Mammoth Lakes. Obsidian is volcanic rock that has cooled so rapidly that the molecules of the chemicals in it have not had the opportunity to separate and orient themselves into mineral components. The rapid cooling of the lava produces a vitreous glass that, when broken, makes the very sharp edge so sought after by Native Americans as a tool useful for cutting, scraping, and penetrating. You might see a broken piece of partially completed arrowhead in one of these workshop areas, but most finished arrowheads discovered in the forest are found by mere chance in places not otherwise associated with old campsites. **Remember: Archaeological sites are protected by federal law. Unauthorized digging and/or collecting of artifacts is prohibited, and violators face heavy penalties.**

Evidence of seasonal use of the area by Native Americans

14.9 (0.1) Forest Road 5S88 goes south ½-mile to the Minarets Pack Station at the edge of Miller Meadow. They offer spot trips or full service trips into the Madera Lakes basin, the Cora Lake country north of Clover Meadow, and the Minarets region of the Ansel Adams Wilderness. They also go into the southern Yosemite region. Having a packer take you into the backcountry allows you to experience the grand High Sierra wilderness that you might otherwise not be able to do on your own. To make advance preparations for such an outing, they can be contacted at Minarets Pack Station, P.O. Box 15, O'Neals CA 93645, (559) 868-3405. Check them out through www.highsierrapackers.org. Even if you don't want to make a backcountry trip right away, stop in and say hello. You can see little flakes of worked obsidian in the parking area in front of the main building. **Remember: no collecting!**

The Minarets Pack Station under construction in the 1950s. The building was erected over a rock outcrop containing bedrock mortars. (Jack Gyer Collection, Fresno Flats Historical Park)

15.1 (0.2) Notice the low cliff of dark rocks on the right side of the road. This lone outcrop is an example of some of the youngest igneous rocks in the Sierra Nevada. The rock is trachybasalt, a type of lava that oozed out of a volcanic vent during the Pliocene Epoch only three to five million years ago. It once covered a large part of this portion of the byway, but something happened a million years ago to change that. During the Pleistocene Epoch, great sheets of ice moved south off the peaks along the southern boundary of Yosemite National Park. Similar to a giant bulldozer, the ice slowly ground over everything in its path, rounding off mountaintops and smoothing out the landscape like a road grader. After the ice melted for the last time, much of the lava was no longer there. This outcrop of trachybasalt is the northernmost exposure of a couple of square miles hidden beneath the forest soil between Miller Meadow and Jackass Meadow.

As you look at this prominent outcrop, notice how it has formed into vertical columns. This is a cooling phenomenon occasionally found in lavas such as basalt and andesite. Perhaps the best-known example of this feature is but a few miles farther up the San Joaquin River at the Devil's Postpile National Monument.

An outcrop of dark trachybasalt along the scenic byway just west of
Miller Meadow displays vertical columns developed during cooling.

Simplified Sierra Nevada Geology

There are three major rock types in the Sierra Nevada. The oldest rocks are
the various sediments that were here long before the Sierra Nevada batholith
pushed its way to the surface. These rocks are at least 150 million years old,
many of them even older. They have all been metamorphosed (changed by
heat and pressure) over the eons of time, so that they no longer resemble their
original characteristics. Except for a dozen or more scattered roof pendants,
these old metamorphic rocks are found mainly along the Mother Lode belt
of the western foothills.

By far the predominate rocks in the Sierra Nevada are the granite-like
crystalline igneous rocks so wonderfully exposed in the cliffs surrounding
Yosemite Valley and along the Tioga Pass Road. The molten rocks were
formed deep within the earth, and were pushed up during the late Jurassic
through the Cretaceous Periods some 65 to 100 million years ago.

Finally, we have the relatively recent igneous rocks, the lava, ash, and other
volcanic rocks that poured out of the earth on top of the granite during the
Tertiary Period only 2 to 15 million years ago. They dominate the landscape
in some places, as on the roads over Sonora and Carson Passes. In others,
they have been eroded by subsequent Pleistocene glaciation, and are scarcely
noticed. This little corner of Madera County is one of those places.

16.3 (1.2) Slow down, and be careful crossing this narrow bridge over Norris Creek. The stream has its headwater at tiny Norris Lake, about two miles to the northwest.

16.6 (0.3) Look to the right for a nice view of the peaks separating Yosemite National Park and Sierra National Forest. From left to right, those peaks are 10,508' Madera Peak, which is entirely within the national forest, and 10,552' Sing Peak and 10,693' Gale Peak on the crest of the ridge. The rocks on the summits of all these high points are composed of old volcanic rocks that were subsequently altered by heat and pressure as granodiorite was being pushed up beneath them.

Chittenden Lake beneath
10,552' Sing Peak

Flat Lake beneath
10,693" Gale Peak

(Dan Carter photos)

16.8 (0.2) Forest Road 5S05 goes north for two miles, where it ends at the Fernandez Trailhead. [Elevation 7,600'] This outstanding trail goes northwest for about seven miles into a glacially carved basin containing more than a half-dozen lakes. The trail then continues over Fernandez Pass [Elevation 10,175'] into Yosemite National Park and the watershed of the South Fork of the Merced River.

Continuing on the byway a hundred yards or so beyond Road 5S05, Road 5S86 to the right leads to the Norris Trailhead [Elevation 7,600']. From here, trails go west into the Jackass Lakes basin [Elevations 8,800'- 9,200'] and northwest into the Madera Lakes basin [Elevations 8,800'- 9,200']. None of these beautiful lakes is difficult to reach, and all are suitable for day hikers.

17.3 (0.5) Forest Road 5S284 on the left goes into the Bowler Group Campground [Elevation 7,100'], which has a capacity of 150 people. Sanitation is by vault toilets, but there is no water. Reservations are not needed.

17.6 (0.3) Trailhead parking for Jackass Lakes is located here. This is the shortest trail into the popular Jackass Lakes basin. The trail is only a couple of miles long, but it involves a steep ascent of 1,000 feet, before crossing the ridge to descend into the basin below.

18.0 (0.4) For the next couple of miles, the striking exposure of bare rock on the right is called "The Balls." When the Pleistocene glaciers rumbled across this area of metamorphic bedrock, all the soil was stripped away, leaving only bare rock. In the 12,000 years since the ice melted, only small patches of soil have developed, not nearly enough to support the usual forest growth. Jeffrey pines have gained a foothold in a few cracks, but, for the most part, the great expanse of rock remains barren. But look at the small patches of sandy soil at the base of The Balls. The small plants growing here are the Sierra stonecrop *Secum obtusatum*. This succulent is found throughout the Sierra Nevada on rocky slopes from 5,000 to 13,000 feet. Its close cousin the Pacific stonecrop *Sedum spathuliolium* prefers shaded and often moss covered rocks at a lower elevation. Both species open the pores in their leaves at night in order to gather the carbon dioxide needed for photosynthesis, the food making process. However, those same pores are closed to conserve moisture during the day.

The yellowish-green growths on the rocks themselves are a kind of lichen called Cumberland rock shield *Xanthoparmella cumberlandia*. They are fungi that have combined with single cell algae to form a new organism. Lichens are highly resistant to cold, drought, and strong sunlight, and since lichens are among the first plants to grow on bare rock, they play a role in soil formation by slowly etching the rock surface.

A hardy Jeffrey pine grows out of a thin crack at The Balls.

Sierra stonecrop

Cumberland rock shield is a lichen commonly
seen growing on bare rock in the Sierra Nevada.

18.3   (0.3) **Stop #5 Jackass Meadow Viewpoint** [Elevation 7,000']

Park in the parking area on the left, and take the level 400-foot trail (wheelchair
accessible) out to a viewing platform overlooking Jackass Meadow, a popular
spot for photographers. As you walk along the boardwalk, notice the forest
trees around you. The predominate tree here is the Ponderosa pine *Pinus
ponderosa*. It has long needles in clusters of three, and it produces a medium
size cone. At the edge of the meadow, the Lodgepole pine often predominates,
as it is more tolerant of wet and poorly drained soils. The Lodgepole pine
Pinus contorta subsp. *murrayana* is easily recognized by its thin bark, short
needles in clusters of two, and relatively small cone. The Lewis and Clark
Expedition of 1804 named the trees 'Lodgepole', when they saw the Native
Americans using their straight, slender trunks in construction of their lodges
and tepees. Other trees to be seen along the path include a few Sierra junipers
Juniperous occidentalis, seemingly out of place here, because they generally
prefer dry rocky slopes in full sun. They can be recognized by their shaggy
bark, their very juniper-looking needles, and their distinctive blue colored
berries. Finally, once at the viewing platform, you can see a few Jeffrey pines
Pinus jeffreyi. This tree also seems a little out of place here, because it likes to
grow among the sage on the eastern slopes of the Sierra Nevada. It is similar
to the Ponderosa in that it has long needles in clusters of three. However,
the cone of the Jeffrey is larger than its cousin the Ponderosa, and the little
prickle at the end of the cone scale turns in, not outward like the Ponderosa.
To remember that important difference, remember the old forester's saying as
he held a cone in his hand: *Gentle Jeffrey, Prickly Ponderosa.*

Although ranchers have been grazing their cattle here for well over 100 years, much of the meadow is private land owned by the Southern California Edison Company. For more than forty years, that company has looked at the site as a potential reservoir for hydroelectric purposes, but there are no current plans to develop the site. The post with a cross-arm on the top was put in by the USFS to serve as a perch for raptors looking for lunch.

The meadow is teeming with life of every kind, from the small aquatic insects that inhabit the wetlands to the occasional deer and coyote who pass through. If you do not see any movement during the daylight hours, come back after dark with a lantern. The Deer mice, Western jumping mice and other small rodents, such as Pocket gophers, are counted by the hundred per acre.

There is a rich diversity of flora here as well, primarily sedges, grasses and forbes. You cannot tell the difference? Again remember the old forester's adage: *Sedges have edges, and grasses, like lasses, are well rounded.* Forbes are the leafy plants growing amid the grasses and sedges.

Early in the summer for well over 100 years, Madera County cattlemen have been driving their cows up into the high country to cow camps in the lush meadows, and bringing them back down to the foothill pastures at the first sign of the coming winter each fall.

Jackass Meadow

At the Turn of the Twentieth Century, a horse trail from Jackass Meadow to Clover Meadow to Soldier Meadow marked the approximate southern boundary of Yosemite National Park. Jackass and Clover Meadows were just outside the park, while Soldier Meadow was just inside. The actual boundary was not surveyed or otherwise marked. It was the U.S. Army whose Cavalry troops patrolled the park at that time, primarily to keep the sheepherders out. Cattle were not welcome in the national park either, but they were not perceived as being as big a problem as the sheep that indiscriminately devoured the vegetation. Old time cowboys like John O'Neal told stories about how he and his new bride, the former Harriet Jones, an accomplished horsewoman herself, were grazing cattle up here. In the absence of any natural or physical barriers, their cows sometimes wandered into the park. The white U.S. Cavalry soldiers had been mean and obnoxious, giving cattlemen a real hard time when the strays were discovered in the park. After 1899 when black troops had begun to patrol the backcountry, a platoon of these "Buffalo Soldiers" proved to be very helpful to the cattlemen in getting their animals back where they belonged.

19.5 (1.2) **Stop #6 Portuguese Creek** [Elevation 7200']

Pull off and stop for a moment in the parking area to the left. From here there is a great view to the south down the Portuguese Creek drainage. From this vantage point, there is also an expansive vista to the southwest of 8,362' Little Shuteye Peak, and to the south of 8,351' Shuteye Peak. Yes, "Little" Shuteye Peak is actually eleven feet higher than Shuteye Peak! Willow meadow can be seen through the trees on the left.

You may also be fortunate to see a peregrine falcon *Falco peregrinus,* an endangered bird that uses the up drafts here along the steep slope to land on the tree or mountain tops. From there, he can spot his primary prey, smaller birds flying below him that are vulnerable to attack. Capable of flying 65 mph in horizontal flight, he can attain speeds approaching 200 mph when executing a dive! The peregrine falcon can be identified by its very long wings that taper down to sharp tips.

23.2 (3.7) A road on the right goes a short distance to Upper Chiquito Campground [Elevation 7,100'], a popular campground where half of the 20 campsites are suitable for trailers. Although it is on the East Fork of Chiquito Creek, no potable water is provided.

23.5 (0.3) Slow down while crossing this narrow bridge over Chiquito Creek. This watercourse flows south out of Chiquito Lake less than three miles to the northwest. A hiking trail up the creek crosses Chiquito Pass [Elevation 8,000'], an easy route into Yosemite National Park.

24.4 (0.9) **Stop #7: Globe Rock** [Elevation 7152']

At first glance, some might think that this round boulder precariously perched on top of an outcrop of bare rock is a glacial erratic, dropped here when the ice retreated; but, it is not. The mineral composition of the granodiorite of the round ball on top is identical to the bedrock beneath it.

Indeed, close examination of the base of the sphere shows feldspar minerals in the bedrock run right up into the globe, thus proving the ball and the base originally were one single piece. Nevertheless, it certainly appears that the round globe is perched there precariously, and could roll off at any moment. That may indeed happen some day, but for the moment they are going nowhere.

So, if this is not a glacial erratic, what caused this geologic oddity? Like Arch Rock, which is of the very same geologic formation, the Mt. Givens granodiorite, the sphere is the product of erosion along joints and cracks, coupled with thousands of years of weathering.

Globe Rock is a corestone produced by erosion.

For Native Americans, this place may have held some special magic. At the very least, it was a summer campsite, as evidenced by the grinding holes worn down into the bedrock near the base of the Globe Rock, where acorns were pounded into meal for baking. The adjoining meadow was probably another summer campsite.

For some years there has been a photo floating around that seems to show President Teddy Roosevelt, and other men, posing for the camera in front of Globe Rock. It is very true that in May of 1903, President Roosevelt came by the Southern Pacific Railroad from San Francisco to the end of the line in the little town of Raymond, (north of Madera), where he greeted the crowd of about 1,500 people who had come to see him. After making a speech, he was taken by stagecoach through Grub Gulch and Ahwahnee and on to Yosemite, where he stayed for several days talking to John Muir. At the end of his visit, he is thought to have returned by the same route to catch another train.

Retired National Park Service historian Jim Snyder says that the President's stay in the park was well documented. He doubts that Mr. Roosevelt would have had time on his return trip to Raymond for an out of the way horseback trip to Globe Rock. The repository for the Roosevelt presidential papers is at the Harvard University library. Archivist Wallace Dailey admits the resemblance of the person in the photo to Mr. Roosevelt, but concludes it is not him. He reports that he can find no record or reference of Roosevelt visiting Globe Rock. Nevertheless, that pesky photograph looks genuine, and it made its appearance years before the modern digital technology of today that has the ability to put anyone anywhere. Did Theodore Roosevelt visit Globe Rock, either during or after his presidency? Your guess is as good as ours!

Is the second man from the left in the foreground
President Theodore Roosevelt?
(Charles Reed collection, courtesy Mildred Reed)

24.9 (0.5) The badly worn section of previously-oiled road ends, and a high standard asphalt surface now resumes.

26.1 (1.2) The buildings to the left at the edge of Muglers Meadow are part of a summer ranch situated on privately owned land. The meadow is named for Christopher Mugler, a Merced River sheepman who used it as his base camp each summer, when he drove his stock into the high mountains to forage. It is estimated that during the drought years in the late 19th Century, as many as 500,000 sheep were grazing in the Sierra Forest Reserve. Competition for the life-sustaining vegetation in the meadows often led to range wars with the cattlemen. While grazing permits are still issued by the US Forest Service to cattlemen, sheep are no longer permitted to graze there, because of the destructive nature of their eating habits.

Should you pass this way in late summer, be watchful along the next couple of miles of the scenic byway for purple elderberries hanging down in massive clusters from the branches of a seven to eight-foot high shrub. Elderberries were a favorite of the Native Americans and early pioneers. They can be made into jelly, baked in pies and cobblers, and even fermented into wine. The picking of a reasonable quantity for personal use is permitted.

The white blossoms of the Elderberry turn into
delicious bluish berries by late summer.

30.4 (4.3) Forest Highway 7 now crosses a bridge spanning Beasore Creek. The creek and meadow derive their name from John Porter Beasore, who ran cattle in this country well over 125 years ago. An early pioneer settler in the Coarsegold area, he had crossed the plains from Iowa in a covered wagon.

30.5 (0.1) The narrow, but paved Grizzly Meadow Road comes in from the left (from mile point 0.0 at the start of this segment).

30.9 (0.4) On the right at the edge of Beasore Meadow is the Jones Store, a local landmark where cold drinks and meals can be obtained.

As you may recall from our description of John French's trail to Mammoth City, Beasore Meadow was the first night's stopping place, where in 1879 French built a cabin in which to house his paying customers. But there is more to the history of this mountain meadow.

Designed to encourage western settlement, the Swamp and Overflow Act was passed by Congress at the same time California was admitted to the Union, making an easy way for old-timers to obtain acreage. Using a team of horses to pull a flat wagon with a boat on it, they would drive through the lush meadows, vouch that they had traversed the area in a rowboat when filing a claim on the land, and it then belonged to them. That is how the private land at Beasore, Arnold and Jackass Meadows was acquired.

Born in Fresno Flats (now Oakhurst) in 1860, John Beasore's son Tom was raised with Tom Jones, another boy about his same age, and they developed a close bond. Each boy had one parent who was an Indian. Beasore filed a claim on the mountain meadow now known as Beasore Meadow.

Around the Turn of the 20th Century, Tom Beasore opened a little store at the edge of the meadow to sell provisions and supplies to the cattlemen who grazed their cows in the nearby meadows each summer. Hot home-cooked meals were also provided as an alternative to the beans and bacon diets of the local cowboys.

In 1923, the cow path coming from Soquel Meadow was turned into a rough dirt road and automobiles could now reach Beasore Meadows and its little store. During the mid-1930s, the Forest Service built the "Beasore Road" up from Bass Lake using Civilian Conservation Corps crews, and within a couple of years it was extended all the way to Clover Meadow. That brought increased automobile traffic into the area, so Tom Beasore had a "Globe" hand-cranked gravity flow gasoline pump installed. In 1938 he also added a western style false storefront to the little store. The original store burned, but in 1954 the present day store was built on the same site.

Having never married, Tom Beasore specified in his will that should he die before his good friend Tom Jones, that Jones would inherit the meadowland pasture. When Tom Beasore died in 1952 at the age of 92, Jones was still alive! Per Beasore's wishes, the land transferred to Jones.

Tom Beasore 1939
(Fresno Flats Historical Park photo)

Yesterday and Today at the Jones Store

Tom Beasore at his store in 1939
(Fresno Flats Historical Park photo)

The Jones Store in the early 1940s
(photo courtesy of Virginia Alberta)

The old gas pump
at the Jones Store

The Jones Store today

A friendly crowd awaits lunch

78

After Tom Jones' death in 1956, the store passed to Vern Black, the son of Hilda Black Jones from her marriage prior to her union with Tom Jones. Although the electrical power and telephone lines have yet to come to Beasore Meadow, the Jones Store remains open during the summer months, and it is still operated by Vern Black and his wife Lois. The little store (you can purchase a cold drink from the propane refrigerators) and cafe (Lois cooks a great hamburger) have become a local institution. If you want to get Vern talking, ask him about his collection of model airplanes. A decorated World War II pilot, Black can tell you stories until the cows are sent down the mountain each fall.

33.1 (2.2) **Stop #8: Cold Springs Summit** [Elevation 7,308']

This crossroads is the highest point on the Sierra Vista National Scenic Byway. The road to the left goes to a glacially carved, shallow basin, containing tiny Chilkoot Lake, a PG&E reservoir feeding Willow Creek and Bass Lake. It is one mile to the east, and accessible to OHVs only. Forest Highway 7, the "Beasore Road", goes straight ahead and descends to Bass Lake. **The Sierra Vista National Scenic Byway turns to the right here onto Forest Road 6S10X.** Before making that right turn onto Forest Road 6S10X however, we suggest you first park in the parking area on the left (restroom), and take the ¼-mile long footpath down to a viewing platform overlooking Cold Springs Meadow. From here you will be rewarded with a nice view north of Madera Peak [Elevation 10,509']. In the spring the meadow puts on a great wildflower display.

Cold Springs Meadow

In the dry sunny areas of sandy or gravely soils along the path, particularly up near the parking lot, you might keep your eye open for Pussy paws *Calyptridium umbellatum*, a prostrate wildflower with rounded pink blossom clusters radiating out from a central leaf and root mass. This sun-loving little plant is somewhat unique in that it regulates its internal temperature by lifting its flower clusters off the ground during the daytime, then lowering them again at night to catch the warmth still radiating off the soil.

Pussy paws

Optional Early Exit Off the
Sierra Vista National Scenic Byway

If the day is getting late and you wish to return to "civilization" before dark, the Beasore Road straight ahead provides a fast and easy way to return to North Fork (21 miles), or to go to Bass Lake (11.5 miles) or Oakhurst (20 miles). If you exercise this option you will miss: Optional Side trip #7- the opportunity to climb Fresno Dome, Stop #10 - the Fresno Dome Viewpoint, Optional Side Trip #8 - the P-40 crash site, and Optional Side Trip #9 - the giant Sequoia trees at Nelder Grove. However, you can easily return to this point another day to complete the scenic byway. The Beasore Road descends some 3,000 feet, passing the USFS Chilkoot Campground on a pretty little stream of the same name. About 30 minutes later, at a point 11.3 miles from Cold Springs Summit, the Beasore Road comes out on County Road 274 (Malum Ridge Road). Once at Road 274, a left turn will take you back to North Fork in another ten miles. A right turn will take you to the Pines Village on the north shore of scenic Bass Lake (where a market, meals, fuel, and accommodations are all available) or you can proceed on another six miles to Highway 41, where a left turn will put you in downtown Oakhurst in a matter of fifteen minutes. Oakhurst offers a full range of services, including many choices of accommodations and meals.

Sierra Vista National Scenic Byway
Part 4

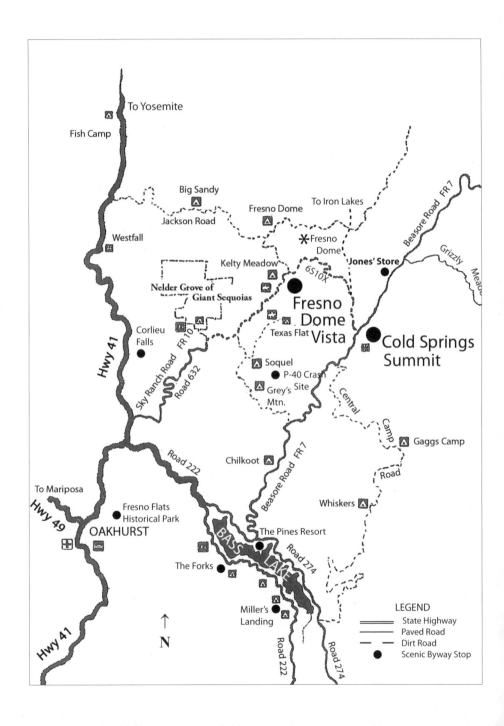

Part 4

Cold Springs Summit To Oakhurst

20.6 miles of paved roadways, half of which are closed by snow from late fall until late spring

This section of the Sierra Vista National Scenic Byway will give the visitor the opportunity to see such natural wonders as Fresno Dome and the Nelder Grove of Giant Sequoia trees. Both of these side trips offer easy trails suitable for the entire family to get out of the automobile and better enjoy the scenery. There is also a bit of history along the way, with the logging of the Sequoia trees in the 1880s, as well as the tragic loss of lives and aircraft during the early days of World War II.

0.0 At Cold Springs Summit, **reset your trip odometer to zero**, and turn west onto Forest Road 6S10X. If you are coming from the north on the byway out of Beasore Meadows, this means you will

turn right. If you are starting the day fresh coming up out of Bass Lake, you will turn to the left. We will follow this secondary forest road for some 5½ miles to the west, where it will join Forest Highway 10. However, if you have not stopped previously, we suggest you first park in the parking area (restroom), and take the ¼-mile long footpath down to a viewing platform overlooking Cold Springs Meadow, where you will be rewarded with a spectacular view of Madera Peak [Elevation 10,509']. In the spring, the meadow is a riot with the colors of wildflowers.

1.4 (1.4) Forest Road 5S39 on the right goes north to connect with roads leading to the Quartz Mountain trailhead (14 miles) and the Iron Lakes jeep trail (7 miles). For a description of the Iron Lakes 4x4 Route, see Optional Side Trip #6 on page 107.

The forest here is predominately Red fir. You may recall reading about this tree back at Arch Rock, Stop #4. Fir and pine are the major conifers in the Sierra Nevada. Of the fir trees, the genus *Abies* is represented by two species, the White fir *A. concolor* and the Red fir *A. magnifica*. Both trees share the same habitat in this part of the Sierra Nevada, from about 5,000' to 8,000' for the White fir and a little higher for the Red fir. Both trees grow to about the same height, up to 200 feet for the White fir and 230 feet for the Red fir, while the trunk diameter of the former is up to four feet, and up to ten feet for the latter. Both species have similar appearing bark, whitish and smooth on young trees and two to four inches thick on mature trees. There are notable differences in the cones, but the easiest way to distinguish between the two trees is by the needles. The White fir has slightly longer needles that are flat and cannot be easily rolled between the fingers. The Red fir has needles that are square shaped in their cross section and can be easily rolled. Some of you may recognize the Red fir as the popular 'silvertip' Christmas tree. Along with the Ponderosa pine and Sugar pine, the Red and White firs make up 80% or more of the forest trees on the western slope of the Sierra Nevada at the middle elevations.

Notice the fluorescent yellow-green "Staghorn moss" growing on the thick bark of the Red fir trees here. Long used by Native Americans as a yellow dye for basket materials and fibers, the growth is not a moss at all, but rather a lichen of the genus *Letharia*. Wolf lichen, as it is sometimes called, clings to the bark of a tree, but it is not a parasite. It takes neither water nor nutrients from its host, but rather uses the tree for support. Whenever you see Wolf lichen on trees, you may notice it seldom grows down low on the trunks. Here the growth seems to start about seven or eight feet above the ground level. Wolf lichen is an "evergreen" in that it grows throughout the year. It needs sunlight to produce chlorophyll, its food. Obviously, the sun does not shine on that part of tree trunks buried in the snow all winter; hence, where this lichen starts growing on the tree trunks is a good indicator of average snow depths in that area.

Wolf lichen on Red fir trees

Wolf lichen is not the only peculiar plant in this part of the forest. Should you pass this way from late May to late June, you are likely to see the bright red stalk of the Snow plant *Sarcodes sanguinea*. Not having any green matter, you might guess that this plant has no chlorophyll; hence it cannot manufacture its own food, and therefore it must be a parasite. Good guess and good reasoning, but your conclusion is only partially correct. The Snow plant is a saprophyte, not a parasite. It obtains its nutrients not from another living organism, but rather from already dead and decaying organic matter. The Snow plant seems to thrive on the forest duff at the base of the Red fir trees, but it is not uncommon in the Ponderosa forest. If you should encounter the Snow plant, leave it alone; **it is protected by state law!**

The Snow plant *Sarcodes sanginea*

2.5   (1.1) Forest Road 6S08 starts off to the left here, in the direction of Texas Flat Campground (8 miles) and Greys Mountain Campground (9 miles). During the post World War II years, a lot of logging has taken place in this part of Sierra National Forest.

Basic Forest Economics

Historically on the Bass Lake Ranger District, the tree with the highest value to be cut has been the Sugar pine. Its wood has few knots, and it has long been sought after to make building lumber. Douglas fir also makes good building material but, here in the central Sierra Nevada, there are relatively few stands and, what trees there are, usually grow on steep north-facing slopes that are hard to reach.

The next species down the economic food chain is Ponderosa pine. It is less desirable than Sugar pine, but Sierra National Forest has lots of it. However, with the formerly nearby mills in Auberry, Cedar Valley, Dinuba, Madera, North Fork, and Oakhurst now closed, the cost to move cut timber all the way to the mills in Sonora or Terra Bella is prohibitively expensive.

The giant Sequoia trees were cut in Nelder Grove in the 1880s and 90s, but the soft wood tended to shatter when the trees fell, resulting in a lot of waste. Thankfully, the biggest trees were spared, because they were bigger than the saw blade could cut. No Sequoia trees have been cut in Nelder Grove in the last 100 years, (the only other Sequoia grove in Sierra National Forest, the McKinley Grove, has never been cut at all). In the absence of Sequoia wood, and the reduction in Coastal redwoods being cut, more Incense cedar is being logged. Like redwood, it holds up well when exposed to the weather, and is commonly used for backyard fences. Cedar prices have remained steady.

Near the bottom of the economic scale are the red and white firs, other soft woods generally unsuitable for building material. Traditionally fir has been used in California to make fruit boxes, but other man-made materials are replacing fir boxes.

Billions of board feet of lumber have come out of Sierra National Forest in the last 130 years. There have been two periods of boom, followed by two periods of bust. The first boom was about 50 years long, from the 1880s to the 1930s. Then the nation's Great Depression pretty much shut down the timber industry. In the 1950s the Congress instructed the Forest Service to step up timber production in order to meet the growing needs for housing by soldiers and sailors returning home from the war. This sparked the second boom period. The allowable cut was increased steadily through the 1950s and 60s, peaking in the 1970s. In 1980 the amount of timber cut varied between 120 and 140 million board feet annually. Beginning in the early 1990s that figure began to drop drastically, and the second "timber depression" set it. During fiscal year 2007/08, the projected cut will be around 14 million board feet, about 10% of what it was 25-30 years ago. With that reduction, most of the mills have closed, and thousands of jobs have been lost forever. This second decline has been caused by a number of factors, including the environmental lobby's attempts to block logging and new forest road construction, coupled with their endless demands on Congress to set aside new Wilderness areas. The ever-increasing costs of labor and diesel fuel have also been important factors. Will timber production once again be an important element in the economy of the Western States, where most of this nation's national forests are? From the present day perspective, it seems unlikely.

4.3   (1.8) Willow Creek flows through a culvert beneath the road. This is the same Willow Creek that flows into Bass Lake, and then on through North Fork.

5.1   (0.8) Road 6S10X now ends at a 'T' intersection with Forest Highway 10. The Sierra Vista National Scenic Byway goes to the left. However, before making that turn to the south, you may wish to consider turning right for a walk to the top of Fresno Dome (see Optional Side Trip #7 described on page 108).

If you choose to continue on the scenic byway, turn left. You will immediately notice that Forest Highway 10 was built to a higher standard, and is in better condition than Forest Road 6S10X that you just left. The byway now generally heads back down towards lower elevations.

5.5   (0.4) The entrance to Kelty Meadows Campground [Elevation 5,800'] is on the right. This popular 27-unit campground has running water, flush toilets, and a campground host to oversee things. A modest fee is charged for camping. Advance reservations can be made by calling (877) 444-6777 or online at www.reserveusa.com.

6.1   (0.6) **Stop #9 Fresno Dome Vista** [Elevation 5600'].

If you did not elect to take Optional Side Trip #7 to Fresno Dome, by all means turn left into the parking lot here; stop for a moment and look to the north. The bare giant monolith protruding through the trees to the north is 7,540' Fresno Dome. It is a prominent local feature that can be seen from the Oakhurst area.

7.0   (0.9) The old wooden barn on the right sits on private property at the edge of pretty Soquel Meadow. Ranchers have been grazing cattle here for well over 100 years.

Soquel Meadow circa 1911
(Fresno Flats Historical Park photo)

To the left, on the edge of the North Fork of Willow Creek sat the Soquel sawmill. In the late 1870s, the Madera Flume and Trading Company had been cutting timber around Gooseberry Flat, turning it into rough lumber at their nearby California Mill, and then sending it down a 54-mile-long flume to Madera. The flume grade was one inch in every sixteen feet or 27 feet in a mile, and it took seven million board feet of lumber just to build it! By 1881, the company wanted to expand their operations with a second sawmill. They found one for sale in the town of Soquel in the coast range above Santa Cruz. The company purchased and laboriously hauled it here by ox driven wagons. The name "Soquel" seems to have been transported here with the machinery, because when the mill was reassembled, it became known as the Soquel Mill, and this idyllic place became Soquel Meadow. The flume was extended farther north, and throughout the summer the Soquel Mill was sending cut lumber down the flume to Madera at a rate of 11.5 million board feet per year. During that same year, the company also established yet another sawmill, California Mill #2, just two miles to the west in the Nelder Grove of big trees.

The Soquel Mill shortly after it opened in 1881
(Madera County Historical Society photo)

In order to feed the voracious appetite of the sawmills, the MF&T
Company experimented in the use of narrow gauge steam trains to carry
the cut trees to the mill. A small seven-ton, four-wheel steam engine was
purchased, disassembled, and hauled here on wagons pulled by oxen. The
plan was a success. For the next several years, narrow gauge rails ran
throughout this portion of the forest, so that the little steam engine "Betsy"
could haul timber to the Soquel Mill.

Betsy, 'the little engine that could'
(Fresno Flats Historical Park photo)

88

8.0   (1.0) Slow down and use extra caution crossing this narrow bridge. The little creek beneath the bridge is a tributary to the North Fork of Willow Creek.

8.2   (0.2) Forest Road 6S40 to the left is an alternative route to Greys Mountain Campground. It also leads to Optional Side Trip #8, the site described on pages 112-113, where a P-40 fighter aircraft crashed on October 24, 1941, tragically killing its pilot.

9.8   (1.6) Forest Road 6S47Y on the right goes to the Nelder Grove of Giant Sequoia trees. If it is too late in the day to take this side trip, be sure to come back at a time when you can spend several hours walking amongst these magnificent old trees. See Optional Side Trip #9 on pages 114 to 120.

10.5 (0.7) Forest Road 6S11 on the left (recommended for high clearance vehicles only) goes out to Bass Lake Vista, a stunning highpoint overlooking the lake. Continue to follow Forest Highway 10, which soon passes Gooseberry Flat, the site of the California Mill No. 1 that operated from 1873 to 1881.

In the late 1990s and early into the 21st Century, you may have heard a lot of talk about the destruction of forest trees by bark beetles, particularly in the San Bernardino Mountains of Southern California. The devastation by insects was bad in the Sierra Nevada as well, particularly during the rainfall year of July 1, 2003 to June 30, 2004, when California experienced a severe drought. Under these unusually dry conditions, the trees, particularly the pines, were greatly stressed and lost much of their natural immunity to fight insect infestations. The Western pine beetle *Dendroctonus brevicomis* wreaked havoc among the Ponderosa pines here. The damage is done when the beetle flies from one infected tree to another, boring through the bark to lay its eggs. The emerging larvae then bore tunnels into the cambian layer beneath the bark in search of food. Normally the sap in the tree retards this tunnel boring process, but when the tree is stressed by drought, little sap is produced. Under these circumstances, the beetle larvae tunnels become so extensive that they often girdle the tree, disrupting its ability to move moisture and food through the cambian layer, and the tree dies.

Fortunately rainfall year 2004/05 saw near record amounts of precipitation in the mountains, and 2005/06 has been above normal as well. The natural immune systems of the trees were able to recover somewhat. Nevertheless, silvaculturists claim that even in years of normal moisture, every conifer tree in the Sierra Nevada is attacked by one or more species of bark beetles, and that these insects kill more forest trees every year than all other natural agents, including forest fires!

Evidence of the Western Pine beetle lies
beneath the bark of this Ponderosa pine.

11.7 (1.2) Forest Road 6S97 on the right goes to Calvin Crest, a privately owned Christian camp that is open year-around.

13.3 (1.6) The thick conifer forest is left behind as Forest Highway 10 now begins to descend in earnest down the dry south-facing hillside. Live oaks and other drought tolerant vegetation dominate the landscape here. The rounded mountain to the south is 4,500' Deadwood Peak. At its northern base sits the town of Oakhurst, surrounding the junction of State Highways 41 and 49.

15.4 (2.1) The first houses now begin to appear on the right, signaling the rapid approach of "civilization." Here Forest Highway 10 becomes known as Sky Ranch Road.

16.3 (0.9) Sky Ranch Road crosses Lewis Creek on a new bridge completed in 2005. Over the years, the open area on the right has been used as pasture land, a sawmill lumberyard, and a golf course. As you cross the bridge you may get a glimpse of the rusting chip burner off to the right. The first sawmill was built here in 1935, but the large metal incinerator was not installed until the late 1940s, when Claude Neely bought it from the long defunct Sugar Pine Mill just six miles up Lewis Creek, and reassembled it here. Its purpose was to burn unwanted sawdust, wood chips, bark, and the outer edges of logs. The mill shut down in 1970, and the burner has been cold ever since. At one time there were a number of these old metal structures in Madera County. This is one of only two still standing.

The old chip burner of the Neely mill has been cold since 1970.
(Fresno Flats Historical Park photo)

16.4   (0.1) On the left is Sierra Sky Ranch, a hostelry and restaurant. Centuries ago, Native Americans recognized what a pleasant place this little valley was, situated alongside Lewis Creek among the oaks and pines. Creek-side grinding holes and the many arrowheads found in the area attest to man's presence long before the coming of white men. But the new settlers did come in with the arrival of William Gash in 1881. The property changed hands several times, but was always used primarily as a ranch until World War II, when the ranch house was pressed into service as a Rest and Recreation Center for American servicemen. In 1946, the facility, including the original ranch house, was converted to a hostelry and renamed "Sierra Sky Ranch." It has served in that capacity for the last 50 years.

Sierra Sky Ranch in the 1970s, when it had a golf course
(Fresno Flats Historical Park photo)

16.5 (0.1) You will now come to a 'T' intersection with busy State Route 41. A right turn here will take you to Fish Camp (11 miles) and the south entrance to Yosemite National Park (13 miles). A turn to the right is also required for Optional Side Trip #10, a hike on the Lewis Creek Trail to pretty little Corlieu Falls (see pages 121 to 126). Turn to the left, and you will soon be in the busy mountain community of Oakhurst, where all services are available.

17.2 (0.7) Road 222 (Bass Lake Road) on the left goes to beautiful Bass Lake (4½ miles) where you can find food, accommodations, picnic areas and campgrounds along Road 222 on the southwest shore, and food, overnight accommodations and an RV park on the northeast shore along Road 432 (North Shore Road). Optional Side Trip #11 on pages 127 to 131 describes the road to Bass Lake. For Oakhurst, continue straight ahead on Highway 41.

18.3 (1.1) The Yosemite Sierra Visitors Bureau on the left is a good place to stop and inquire about the wide range of accommodations available in Oakhurst, from national chain motels, to Bed and Breakfast accommodations, to the five-star Chateau de Sureau. They are open daily from 8:30 a.m. to 5 p.m. Monday-Saturday and 9-1 Sundays. There is also an "after hours" information board with direct toll-free telephone connections for local lodging.

20.3 (2.0) Here on the left, at the intersection of Highway 41 and Road 426 (Crane Valley Road) in downtown Oakhurst, is what locals call the "Talking Bear." See for yourself, if you want to talk to the bear. Newspapers world-wide have done stories on the talking bear, so don't be surprised to find a European tourist here trying to talk to the bear in German or French, or heavily accented English.

If you have elected to drive the entire Sierra Vista National Scenic Byway in one day, this will be the first traffic signal that you have encountered in well over 100 miles!

20.6 (0.3) The commercial heart of Oakhurst is right here at the intersection of State Highways 41 and 49, at the southern tip of California's "Mother Lode" country. Besides having several large chain grocery and drug stores, there are a half-dozen motels in town, and several dozen places to eat. Your dining choices range from national fast food outlets, several pizza parlors and coffee shops, restaurants offering ethnic menus, such as Mexican, Chinese, and Japanese cuisine, to even one world-renowned five-star restaurant, Erna's Elderberry House.

Originally called Fresno Flats, a small community developed in the 1850s to supply fresh meat, fruits and vegetables to the hungry miners panning gold out of Coarsegold Creek. Eventually the auriferous gravels were worked out, and the attention turned to hard rock mines of nearby

Texas Flat, Potter Ridge and Grub Gulch. Now the miners needed not only sustenance, but also timber to shore up their underground tunnels. Again, Fresno Flats answered the call, supporting not only the miners, but loggers working in the forests high above the little town. Ranchers from the lower foothills drove their cattle through Fresno Flats twice a year in their annual migration to and from the high meadow pasturelands. In 1874 logging took on major proportions, when the California Lumber Company began to set up a large sawmill at the 5,600' level on California Creek, and began construction of a 54-mile long V-shaped flume to be used to float the cut lumber down to the Southern Pacific Railroad at Madera in the San Joaquin Valley. The flume ran right through Fresno Flats. By 1884 there were 200 people in the little community of Fresno Flats that boasted two stores, two hotels, a blacksmith, a skating rink and dance hall, the first school in Madera County, and three saloons.

For 55 years, from 1877 to 1932, this 54-mile long flume carried cut lumber from the mill down through Fresno Flats and on to the railroad in Madera. (Photo courtesy of Fresno Flats Historical Park)

When, in 1912, the local citizenry decided that the name "Fresno Flats" did not project the proper ambience for their community, they changed the name to Oakhurst.

The great depression years of the 1930s were hard on everyone, and sawmills all over the West closed. But after World War II, all the returning soldiers and sailors were getting married, creating the need for new houses. The U.S. Forest Service responded by opening new areas in the forest to logging. In 1947, Oakhurst got its own sawmill. It operated at a site now occupied by the Old Mill Shopping Center, where Longs Drugs and Vons are located.

The shopping center where Vons and Longs are now
located was a sawmill between 1947 and 1980.
(Fresno Flats Historical Park photo)

During this same period, the modest land values in Oakhurst had been attracting retirees coming from the large metropolitan urban areas, so when the sawmill closed in 1980, the community easily survived the loss of local jobs. Today the economic health of Oakhurst is good, and in spite of nagging water problems, the community's future seems bright.

For a more complete perspective on Oakhurst's 150 year old past, be sure to stop at the Fresno Flats Historical Park, described in Optional Side Trip #12 on pages 133 to 135. Here a number of historic buildings furnished with period pieces are open daily to visitors. Call (559) 683-6570 for hours of operation.

To return to Fresno or Madera, simply take Highway 41 south out of Oakhurst. The drive to either destination takes less than an hour. It is 45 miles to Fresno, 40 miles to Madera.

Days Gone By in Oakhurst

Fresno Flats as it was around 1890.
The name was changed to Oakhurst in 1912.

This saloon was the center of social life for
many men in Fresno Flats during the 1890s.

Nichols House and Hotel circa 1880
(Fresno Flats Historical Park photos)

Part 5

Optional Side Trips off the Scenic Byway

The Sierra Vista National Scenic Byway offers a complete package of breathtaking scenery, nature, and man's history in the region. In addition, we have described here a dozen side trips that will further enhance your visit to the central Sierra Nevada. Some of these side excursions involve unique natural features, such as Fresno Dome and the Nelder Grove of Big Trees. Others, like Mormon Jimmy's cabin and a visit to the Fresno Flats Historical Park, will place emphasis on man's presence in the mountains. Still others, like the Exact Center of California, are truly unique.

A few of these side trips will involve a little walking, but the trails are short and generally easy. The ascent of Fresno Dome is an example. The giant Sequoia trees of Nelder Grove can be seen without getting out of your car; however, to really experience the wonder of these massive giants, one should certainly take the Shadow of the Giants and/or the Graveyard of the Giants Trails.

Most of these side trips are over paved, or at least graded secondary roads. Two excursions, however, the Rock Creek Falls and the Iron Lakes side trips, involve rough jeep trails, where a high clearance four-wheel drive vehicle is a must. If you have such a vehicle, and are experienced in off-road driving, by all means make these journeys. They will certainly add to the adventure, and provide an experience you would miss by staying on the byway.

Finally, while we have not described them as specific side trips, the Sierra Vista National Scenic Byway leads to trailheads where the day hiker, or backpacker, can access the Ansel Adams Wilderness and all the natural wonders it has to offer.

The Sierra Vista National Scenic Byway is an open door to other places in the central Sierra Nevada, and the person who simply stays on the byway will be missing many nearby features of interest.

Side Trip #1
from page 38
Exact Center of California Monument
Accessible year around

Have you ever lain awake at night, mentally pondering where the exact center of some state is? That is relatively easy to determine for states with rectangular borders, such as Colorado or Wyoming. Simply draw two lines from opposing corners and see where they intersect. With its long curving shape, the solution is not quite so easy for California. Years ago, someone having nothing better to do measured the entire length of Highway 99 from north to south, and determined that the halfway point was near the City of Madera just south of Avenue 11. A palm tree was planted on the south side of the perceived point, and a pine tree planted on the north side. The Madera Chamber of Commerce made plans to erect a monument on the spot, and to promote its importance. Not so fast, however; cooler heads prevailed and thought a more scientific approach was needed.

In 1972 the Madera County Board of Supervisors commissioned a better survey. The County Engineering Department determined the center to be about a mile north of Redinger Dam on the San Joaquin River, just a few miles southeast of North Fork. The exact spot was marked with a metal stake and promptly forgotten. Somehow, over the years, the marker was removed. In 1993, the North Fork History Group resurrected the search for the exact center of California, and they sought assistance, first from the U.S. Forest Service and then from the Engineering and Surveying Department at California State University Fresno. Using modern and sophisticated geo-positioning satellite technology, they determined the exact center of the state. This time, the site was more properly marked and dedicated by representatives from CSUF, the California Department of Transportation, the U.S. Geological Survey, the U.S. Forest Service and, of course, many of the residents of North Fork. Crews from Fresno television stations duly recorded the event, and a documentary was aired on PBS.

To visit the place that was determined to be the exact center of the State of California, turn right on County Road 225 (Italian Bar Road) and proceed 2½ miles to where a USFS sign announces you are entering the Redinger Lake Recreation Area. Just beyond, look to the left for some steps leading up to a stone monument. You will now be able to say that you have been to the exact center of California.

Return to the Minarets Road by the same route. If your odometer is reasonably accurate, you will have to add 5.0 miles to all coming mileages on Part 1 of the scenic byway in order to compensate for this side trip.

97

EXACT CENTER OF CALIFORNIA
LATITUDE 37° 9' 58.23" N
LONGITUDE 119° 26' 58.29" W
DEDICATED NOV. 1998
BY
NORTH FORK HISTORY GROUP

Side Trip #2
from page 44

Mormon Jimmy's cabin and mine
Accessible year around

Turn to the left onto Forest Road 8S27, noting your mileage as you leave the scenic byway. Proceed west on the forest road through a mixed forest of oak, pine and Incense cedar. With care, the road can be driven by standard passenger automobiles. Do not be deterred should you be here during the season when the gate is normally locked; it is still an easy, mostly level walk of less than a mile to the site of Mormon Jimmy's cabin. At a point 0.9 miles off the byway, look for a rough road going up the slope to the right. Stop here, and walk about 50 yards up the hillside to the right. Hidden among the trees and underbrush are the stone walls of an old cabin. Just a few feet to the west is an overgrown and largely collapsed mine tunnel.

There is a tragic story to be told here about one James Lawson and the death of his daughter. Lawson arrived in North Fork in the summer of 1889. He did not smoke or drink and, as he came from Utah, the townsfolk assumed he was of the Mormon faith. The nickname "Mormon Jimmy" was soon bestowed on him, and the name seems to have stuck. History is a little vague at this point, but somewhere along the line Lawson took a wife, and within a year or so they had a daughter. Jimmy also bought a mining claim (shown on maps as the Pine Grove Mine), and built a stone cabin on it to house his family. In order to process the gold ore from the newly acquired mine, Jimmy built an arrastre, a crude device to crush and pulverize the quartz so that the gold could be extracted. The arrastre was powered by a large overshot waterwheel, with the water carried several miles downhill via a ditch coming off Whisky Ridge. (If you explore the nearby area, you can still see remnants of Jimmy's ditch.)

Early in 1900, Jimmy shot and killed his young daughter. Jimmy said he was shooting at some wild animal that he thought was prowling outside the cabin, and that it was an accident. His distraught wife said he shot the little girl in a fit of anger, when she would not stop crying.

Whatever the actual story, Jimmy was arrested and taken to Madera to stand trial. He soon escaped by digging his way out through the dirt floor of the jail. He was eventually recaptured, convicted of manslaughter, and sentenced to San Quentin Prison. Jimmy escaped again when the sheriff transporting him to prison fell asleep, and he quietly walked off the train car when it was stopped in Lodi. After he had been hiding for two days, a barking dog detected his presence, and Jimmy was soon again prison bound. Jimmy was a model prisoner at San Quentin. Three years later he was paroled, when the court found that he had been convicted on the prejudicial testimony of his wife, who had wanted to be off the mountain and away from the long days of hard work.

Mormon Jimmy returned to his home near North Fork, but things were not the same. He had lost his wife, his daughter, and all of his possessions. He made an attempt to work his mine, but his heart was not in it. Ultimately, James Lawson died in a Madera hospital, an old man and a ward of the county.

Sometime while he was in custody, someone entered Mormon Jimmy's cabin and scratched the words M-U-R-D-E-R-E-R in the stone fireplace mantle. A few of those letters are faintly visible today.

Mormon Jimmy's cabin

Side Trip #3
from page 55
Rock Creek Falls

Warning: Do not attempt this excursion unless you are an experienced off-road driver in a high-clearance four-wheel drive vehicle! Having two such vehicles and a tow strap are also highly recommended.

Almost immediately upon entering the Rock Creek Campground, the road splits into three directions. The right and left forks go to campsites within the

campground. The branch going straight ahead is Forest Road 7S47. Follow this road beyond the campground, and you will soon find yourself descending the Rock Creek drainage down into the San Joaquin River gorge. This narrow, but once-oiled road was built and used in the early 1950s as a part of the construction of the eight-mile long tunnel between Mammoth Pool Dam and the Mammoth Pool Powerhouse. The upper couple of miles are still in reasonably good condition, in spite of the fact that no maintenance has been done on the road in the last fifty years. However, **do be watchful for any rocks that may have rolled off the hillside onto the pavement.** Beyond these first few miles, the lower this road descends into the canyon, the worse the road condition becomes.

About four miles below the byway, the asphalt surface ends at a 'T' intersection. The right fork goes ¼-mile over to a small diversion dam just above the waterfalls on Rock Creek. A large boulder that has slid onto the roadway from above now blocks this road. To see the waterfalls from above, you will have to walk the last 100 yards. It's worth the walk.

Take the left fork to get a better view of the Rock Creek Falls. Engage your four-wheel drive, if you have not done so already. There are some very deep ruts in the last ¼-mile that have to be carefully straddled. The road ends on a large, elongated flat bench overlooking the river, just a few hundred vertical feet below. While the large trees and brush growing on this bench may, at first glance, make the scene appear to be natural, it is not. This flat area is actually the top of an enormous tailing dump created when the eight-mile long tunnel between the

Mammoth Pool Dam and its powerhouse was dug out of solid granite. Nearby is the fenced off portal of a connecting tunnel. Beyond the tunnel are nice views south of Rock Creek and the many waterfalls cascading along its lower course.

Once you have had the opportunity to look around and admire the scenery, you must return to the byway by the same route. For the first mile, the ascent is worse than the descent, because you have gravity working against you. **As you come to each washed out section, carefully plan where you want to place your wheels. If necessary, have a passenger get out to guide you ahead.** The trick is to avoid sliding into one of the three-foot deep ruts.

The tunnel portal

Rock Creek Falls

Side Trip #4

from page 61

The Mammoth Pool and Dam

To visit this popular fishing destination, note your odometer, and turn to the right onto Forest Road 6S25. After going 1.4 miles, Forest Road 6S61Y goes off the paved road a half-mile to end at the USFS Placer Campground [Elevation 4,100'], a facility with seven campsites, running water and vault toilets. There is no campground host, but a modest fee is charged.

Continuing on down Road 6S25, another USFS campground is reached at a point 2.3 miles below the byway. This is Sweetwater Campground [Elevation 3,800'], a ten-unit site having seven campsites suitable for trailers. Picnic tables and a vault toilet are provided. Although it is on Chiquito Creek, there is no potable water piped into the campground. Again, a modest fee is charged to camp here.

At a point 3.5 miles below the byway, the pavement ends, to be replaced by two high standard dirt roads. Here a sign points to Forest Road 6S25 continuing on the right, indicating that Mammoth Pool Dam is three miles in that direction. A few hundred feet straight ahead on Forest Road 6S76 is Wagner's Mammoth Pool Resort, a friendly family-oriented place catering to anglers and campers [Elevation 3,500']. During the summer months, they offer a store, café, cabins, trailer park, gasoline and their own campground. Call (559) 841-3736 for information.

Road 6S76 continues on beyond Wagner's, crossing the French Trail 0.4 miles below the resort. Eventually Road 6S76 ends at the reservoir boat launch ramp at a point 5.1 miles below the byway. Fishing can be quite good at Mammoth Pool, with 12 to 16 inch-long rainbows common, and 6 to 10-pound Brown trout not unheard of.

Mammoth Pool Reservoir

If you wish to visit the dam, and it is quite impressive, return to Wagner's Resort and turn left onto the dirt Forest Road 6S25. A sign indicates that the road is closed from May 1st to June 16th of each year to allow the migrating deer herds to swim across the reservoir undisturbed by boaters or fishermen. After passing the pleasant Windy Point Picnic Area, the dirt road crosses the Mammoth Pool Dam and ends on the Fresno County side of the canyon, about 3.4 miles from Wagner's Resort. The view of the inner gorge with its stark granite bedrock is awesome. When the reservoir is full, and water is pouring over the spillway as it does in wet years, the thundering roar is deafening and the ground shakes.

Mammoth Pool Dam while under construction
(Jack Gyer Collection, Fresno Flats Historical Park)

Mammoth Pool Dam today

Mammoth Pool Dam and the reservoir behind it are but one more link in a chain of hydroelectric generating facilities operated by the Southern California Edison Company in the San Joaquin River drainage. Any visitor to the dam must marvel at the skill and engineering in its construction. Even more incredible is the fact that, working 24/7 with floodlights along the canyon walls, this entire construction project took only thirteen months to complete. Years of planning and preparation paid off. The actual construction work began on February 1, 1958, continued through the following winter, and was completed in the spring of 1959. The result was an earth-filled dam that rises 310 feet above the old river bottom, is 870 feet thick at the base and 2000 feet long. The lake behind the dam is eight miles long, and holds 120,000 acre-feet of water. The elevation is 3,330 feet when it is full, with the mountains rising 2000 feet above the lake's surface, and forming a steep narrow valley. The reservoir and dam are named for the large, natural pool in the river that existed here even before the dam was built.

The visitor may notice the absence of generators and high voltage power lines emanating from here. That is because no electricity is directly generated at this site. Instead, water from the San Joaquin River, stored in the Mammoth Pool Reservoir, is funneled into an eight-mile long tunnel down to the Mammoth Pool Powerhouse where, after generating electricity, it is returned to the San Joaquin River (see page 45).

This 18-foot diameter pipe inside the mountain, will deliver water from Mammoth Pool to the powerhouse eight miles down the canyon. Taken in October 1958, this photo shows where the gate-valve will be installed.
(Marilyn Elliott photo, Fresno Flats *Sierra Star* collection)

Side Trip #5
from page 64
Clover Meadow

By turning to the right onto Forest Road 5S30, we can visit a little corner of Sierra National Forest that was once within a larger Yosemite National Park. Note your odometer, and follow the once-oiled road for 1.8 miles; here you will come to the USFS Clover Meadow Ranger Station. Hikers wanting to backpack on overnight trips into the Ansel Adams Wilderness can obtain the necessary permit here. From the ranger station, hiking trails go west about four miles into the beautiful Jackass Lakes and Madera Lakes basins.

The road forks at the Ranger Station. Forest Road 5S30 to the left was originally built in the World War II era to access the Strawberry Tungsten Mine. Tungsten was first found here in 1941 by a couple of local cowboys, Jim McDougald and Dutch Cobb. World War II created a demand for this strategic metal that is used as an alloy to harden steel. In 1943, a road was built into the property, and a 50-ton per day concentrating mill was installed. The mine was worked off and on between 1943 and 1968, producing some 480,000 short-ton-units of tungsten ore. Teledyne Inc. acquired the property in 1976, and worked the deposit for another decade. The mine and 350-tons/day concentrating mill remain private property, with a locked gate preventing access. The Strawberry Mine is located in another one of those metamorphic roof pendants mentioned previously on pages 55 and 56. There are still substantial ore reserves left in the mine, but currently the price of tungsten is depressed, with much of the world's supply coming from China, where it can be extracted for far less than in this remote corner of the Sierra Nevada.

The mine entrance is on the right a mile beyond the Ranger Station, while Forest Road 4S43 goes to the left, where it crosses a bridge and forks again. Road 5S30 to the right now goes on to trailhead parking areas from which backpackers can access Cora Lakes and Isberg Pass, the latter being a relatively little-used route into the back country of Yosemite National Park. The road then goes on to the trailhead parking for the Mammoth Trail that descends to Sheep Crossing on the North Fork of the San Joaquin River, before climbing up to the 77 Coral and the Granite Stairway into the Devil's Postpile National Monument to join the John Muir Trail.

From the Mammoth trailhead parking area, a jeep trail climbs to the top of Cattle Mountain, where there are spectacular views of Balloon Dome and the high country to the east. For a description of the Cattle Mountain OHV route, see *High Sierra SUV Trails, Volume II – The Western Slope.*

Lewis Monkeyflower *Mimulis lewisii*   Coneflower *Rudbeckia californica*

As you explore this area of Clover Meadow, look for the Coneflower *Rudbeckia californica*, easily identified by the two-inch brown cone rising in the center from daisy-like bright yellow petals. A member of the aster family, it likes the moist wetland of the meadow and can grow to be four feet tall here. When in bloom, it is certainly hard to miss.

If you follow Forest Road 4S60 to the right at the Clover Meadow Ranger Station, it will take you to the USFS Granite Creek Campground in a mile. There is no daily charge to stay in this popular campground that has twenty campsites, of which five are suitable for trailers. There is no potable water at the campground. The water in Granite Creek must be treated before using.

The road continues on beyond the campground, but the **fording of Granite Creek is hazardous at best and, if attempted at all, should only be done with four-wheel drive vehicles.**

Side Trip #6

from page 81

Jeep Trail to Iron Lakes

Recommended for four-wheel drive vehicles only

Turn right onto Forest Road 5S39, and proceed north. The road has not been maintained since it was last oiled many years ago, so expect some potholes. After going three miles, you will come out onto Forest Highway 10 (Sky Ranch Road). Stay to the right for another mile; here a sign will point to Forest Road 5S92, and the beginning of the 1½-mile long Iron Lakes OHV Trail. The jeep trail winds its way up a hillside through a forest of Red fir, then crosses a rocky ridge to end overlooking an alpine lake, nestled at the northern base of Iron Mountain. From this vantage point, there are also nice views north of the Buena Vista Crest in Yosemite National Park.

From the end of the road, it is but a short ten-minute walk down to Iron Lake. If you have any doubts as to whether there are any trout in this lake, just walk over to the outlet, and look down into the crystal clear water.

The Iron Lakes Basin consists of four lakes. First, there is tiny Upper Iron Lake, which drains into the much larger Lower Iron Lake. Both of these alpine lakes are tucked in a glacial cirque beneath the reddish metamorphic rocks of 9,165' Iron Mountain. From the lower lake, a foot trail crosses a small glacial moraine and descends a quarter-mile to shallow Junction Lake. From here anglers can follow one trail for 1½ miles down to Grizzly Creek, or take a different trail

Lower Iron Lake

up to Bare Island Lake, another fine fishery. For a more detailed description of this jeep trail, see our companion volume *High Sierra SUV Trails, Volume II – The Western Slope*.

108

Side Trip #7

from page 85

Fresno Dome

An easy to moderate hike of a mile to the top

There are many domes scattered throughout the central Sierra Nevada, the best known of which account for the splendor of Yosemite Valley. John Muir wrote in August 1875:

I caught sight of a lofty dome, called Wa-mello by the Indians, looming into the sky far above the forest. I soon found myself upon its commanding summit . . .

The dome he speaks of is Fresno Dome, and for travelers on the Sierra Vista National Scenic Byway, the site is readily accessible to all who wish to stand on its lofty promontory.

To reach the Fresno Dome trailhead, turn to the right at Forest Road 10, and follow the signs to Quartz Mountain. You will pass the Big Sandy Road to Fish Camp on the left after going 1.6 miles. (After eight miles this road will take you to Fish Camp and State Route 41.) Continuing up Forest Road 10 another tenth of a mile will bring you to the entrance to the popular 15-unit USFS Fresno Dome Campground. Continue following Forest Road 10 for another 2.3 miles, and look for the Fresno Dome Trailhead off to the right. There is adequate parking well off

the roadway. A good hiking trail leaves the trailhead parking area, and makes a vertical climb of about 350 feet in a little over a half-mile. The top of the rock monolith can be easily climbed in 20-30 minutes without undue effort. Allow an hour or a little more for the round trip. Shoes suitable for hiking are recommended.

The view from the 7,540' summit is superb! To the south one can look all the way to downtown Oakhurst and beyond into the San Joaquin Valley. To the northeast is the summit of 9,165' Iron Mountain. To the northwest is

Fresno Dome as seen from its north side.　8,691' Raymond Mountain. To the west in the far distance one can look down into the drainage created by the South Fork of the Merced River.

Climbing Fresno Dome

The Summit

View south looking down upon Deadwood Peak and into the Oakhurst basin

Trees Along the Trail

The Fresno Dome Trail provides the forest visitor with a unique perspective of the various trees to be found along the way. The first tree you are likely to notice upon leaving the parking area is the Quaking aspen *Populus tremuloides*. It has long been a favorite pastime for young lovers and Basque sheepherders to carve their initials into the soft white bark. Early in the summer, its bright green leaves stand out in marked contrast to the dark needles of its forest neighbors. In the fall, it is a tree that simply cannot be ignored. With the shorter days and cooler nights, there is a chemical change in the leaves that causes them to turn from yellow to orange to crimson red.

The trail goes through the deep forest for the first quarter-mile. Here we find the very large Red fir *Abies magnifica* and the somewhat smaller White fir *Abies concolor.* They like well-drained soils. On poorly drained soils around the meadow area, we find the Lodgepole pine *Pinus contorta subsp. murrayana.* Young trees of this two-needle species often have their trunks twisted and contorted under the weight of the winter snows. In the rocks, just beyond the edge of the Red fir-Lodgepole pine forest, keen eyes will spot a few shrub like specimens of Black oak *Quercus kelloggii*. The elevation range of this tree is about 7,000 to 7,500 feet in this part of the central Sierra Nevada. Here at 7,200 feet is about the upper end of its normal habitat range.

As the forest is left behind and the actual climb up the north face of Fresno Dome begins, the trail passes several nice specimens of large Jeffrey Pine *Pinus jeffreyi* that have somehow managed to take root and thrive in the cracks of this granite monolith. Their shade offers a good excuse to pause for a moment, before resuming the final ascent to the top. About fifty yards below the summit, the highest tree to be seen on the rock is a stunted specimen of Whitebark pine *Pinus albicaulis*. If you look closely, you will see that its needles are in groups of five. The harsh environment of this windswept perch has stunted the tree's growth. Its contorted trunk is more than a foot in diameter, but the tree is only about five feet high! This tree likes the inhospitable growing conditions, as it does not have to compete for soil, moisture, and sunlight with other species of trees. Its normal habitat range in the central Sierra Nevada is usually from about 8,000 up to 11,000 feet, so this particular tree is actually growing below the lower end of its normal habitat.

White fir and aspen at the trailhead.

Can you find this Black oak along the trail?

Lodgepole pine often grow in poorly drained soils.

The bark of the Jeffrey pine
smells faintly like vanilla.

Wind and weather have stunted the growth
of this near prostrate Whitebark pine.

Side Trip #8
from page 88

P-40 Crash Site

Turning left on Forest Road 6S40, we quickly come to appreciate just what a fine road Forest Highway 10 is. This once-oiled road has deteriorated in recent years. Without the timber industry to maintain these secondary forest roads, they quickly develop potholes and ruts. Nevertheless, if driven with care, today's automobile should be able to negotiate this road just fine.

After going only 0.4 miles, the entrance to the Soquel Campground [Elevation 5,400'] appears on the left. This 11-unit campground has a host, and a modest fee is charged to stay here. For the P-40 crash site, continue straight ahead on 6S40. Soon there will be views down the slope to the left of the North Fork of Willow Creek flowing past on its way to Bass Lake. After going 1½ miles, Road 6S40 crosses a bridge over the creek, and on the other side, the roads forks, with 6S40 passing the entrance to 26-unit Greys Mountain Campground. However, we are going to go to the left now, taking Forest Road 6S08.

At a point 3.3 miles in from Forest Road 10, look for a logging spur that goes steeply up the hill to the right. About 125 feet beyond the spur, pull off Road 6S08, and park at a wide place on the left. The spot is not marked, other than with some silver duct tape wrapped high around a tree trunk. If you have a GPS receiver, the coordinates at the parking area are N41°29.658 W120°32.461. Lock your car, and walk down the gentle slope about 100 yards. There is no clear path to the crash site, so watch your step, and don't trip over any downed fir tree branches.

The site is marked with a small stone monument placed by the pilot's relatives in 1942, and by a bronze plaque placed in 1996. Nearby is a small depression in the earth with the aircraft's Allison engine protruding out of the hole. This was the place where Army Air Corps Lt. W.H. Birrell crashed, and lost his life. However, there is much more to the story.

On Friday morning, October 24, 1941, just a few weeks before the Japanese bombed Pearl Harbor, a flight of 19 Curtis P-40 Warhawks of the 57th Pursuit Group took off from March Field near Riverside, California, en route to McCord Army Airfield in the State of Washington. While flying over the Sierra Nevada, the fighters encountered bad weather. The pilots, who were flying in formation, had to split up and scatter when the heavy cloud cover prevented them from seeing each other. One plane had engine failure, and the pilot bailed out. Three other aircraft went down over Kings Canyon National Park. One pilot crashed near Tulare. Nine other pilots made forced landings in Nevada, where one plane was destroyed and another badly damaged. Of the 19 aircraft, only four made it to their scheduled refueling stop at McClellan Field near Sacramento.

[handwritten in left margin: N37°34.565 / W119°32.490]

[handwritten note near coordinates: CORRECTED COORDINATES]

Our story revolves around Lt. W.H. Birrell, a 1940 graduate of West Point, who crashed here near Greys Mountain. We do not know if he had an engine failure due to the carburetor icing up, or if he passed out due to lack of oxygen after flying to 16,000 feet trying to get above the clouds. Another scenario was that after failing to fly above the clouds, he next tried to fly under them, and being unable to see anything, he did not realize how close the ground was. Whatever the situation, Lt. Birrell's plane slammed into the forest and burst into flames from the spilled fuel.

Forest Ranger Eldridge Westfall heard the crash from several miles away, but it was not until the following day that a Bass Lake resort owner, flying his own plane, spotted the burned wreckage. There was nothing a ground rescue team could do for Lt. Birrell. He was killed instantly upon impact.

A Curtis P-40 "Warhawk" aircraft of the type Lt. Burrell was flying

The engine block was driven into the ground upon impact, and it remains there to this day.

Side Trip #9

from page 88

Nelder Grove of Giant Sequoia Trees

Only two groves of Giant Sequoia trees are to be found within Sierra National Forest. Indeed, of the 59 groves found in the Sierra Nevada, only seven lie north of the Kings River and, of these, only three are located between the Kings and Merced Rivers. The cluster of Sequoia trees at Nelder Grove covers nearly 500 acres, making it a "mid-size grove", neither the largest nor the smallest. Its nearest neighbor is the slightly larger and never cut Mariposa Grove, just four miles to the north in Yosemite National Park.

The first written reference to these Sequoia trees comes in 1851 as an entry in the diary of Robert Eccleston, a member of the "Mormon Battalion" who passed through here on a punitive expedition chasing local Indians. His entry for April 18, 1851, refers to seeing a noble redwood measuring 60 feet around at the base. In the mid-1850s, another local resident, Galen Clark, may have been the second white man to see Nelder Grove. He told the story that, while on a hunting trip, he heard a tremendous crash in the forest. Upon investigating the sound, he discovered a mighty redwood tree had fallen. To his great surprise, there were hundreds of others nearby. Clark named the area Fresno Grove, for its proximity to the Fresno River.

The California No. 2 mill operated at
Nelder Grove from 1882 to 1892.

Naturalist John Muir first visited the Nelder Grove in 1875 and found a former prospector turned hermit, John Nelder, living there on a 165-acre homestead claim. Muir and Nelder hit it off right away, and Muir spent a week as a guest in

Nelder's cabin. Muir was appalled by the thought of cutting these magnificent trees. Later, in 1890, he lobbied unsuccessfully to have Nelder Grove included in the newly created Yosemite National Park. (Nelder and his deaf cat died in 1889 when his cabin burned, and after that, the trees became known as "Nelder Grove.") In 1892 Nelder's son Claudis sold his father's land to the Madera Flume and Trading Company, which had already been logging Sugar pine from the area for a decade, and were operating the California No. 4 Mill at the north edge of Nelder Grove.

This ingenious gravity operated tram moved cut lumber from the California No. 2 Mill to the Soquel flume that carried lumber to Madera.
(Madera County Historical Society photos)

In 1900 Nelder Grove changed hands again, and this time it was sold to the Madera Sugar Pine Company, whose narrow gauge tracks radiated out of their great mill at Sugar Pine. They, too, built a long flume to transport their cut lumber to the railroad in Madera, and in their early years continued to cut timber around the Nelder Grove area.

This 54-mile long flume carried cut lumber from the Sugar Pine Mill down to Madera.
(Fresno Flats Historical Park photo)

116

There are a lot of Sugar pines mixed in among the Sequoia trees, and it was this species that attracted the loggers in the late 1860s. In 1870 the grand "Forest King" tree was felled by digging the soil out from its base, cutting the roots, and letting the tree topple over by its own unsupported weight. The tree was not used for its lumber, but rather its trunk was sliced into rounds for exhibition purposes. Nevertheless, between 1874 and 1892 some 280 mature Sequoia trees were cut in Nelder Grove. Fortunately, 106 of the larger trees were spared, not because of compassion or any sense of conservation on the part of the loggers, but because the trees were simply too big for the saw blades in the mill to handle.

As you walk the trails in Nelder Grove, you may wonder why the stumps of cut trees are so high above the ground. In those days, Sequoia trees were typically cut by two men standing on raised platforms 10 to 15 feet above the ground, using a crosscut saw. Each man would stand on one side of the trunk, pulling his end of the saw blade while the other man pushed and vice versa. Once the tree fell, the real work began. The tree had to be cut into small enough pieces so that it could be moved to the mill. The loggers were helped by the fact that Sequoia wood is soft and tended to shatter when it fell. Often times, there was a lot of waste, with much of the wood too broken up to be used.

Cutting Sequoias in the 1880s
(Fresno Flats Historical Park photo)

The Forest Service has the turnoff to Nelder Grove well-marked on Forest Highway 10. Turn to the right onto Forest Road 6S47Y, and after 1.2 miles you will come to a 'T' intersection with Forest Road 6S90. Turning to the right on 6S90 will soon bring you to the "historic" part of Nelder Grove, while a left turn onto 6S90 will take you to the *Shadow of the Giants Trail*. (This dirt road eventually goes on to the old mill site and present day community of Sugar Pine, where access can be made to Highway 41 again.) Both parts of Nelder Grove should be visited, but let's first go to the left.

The parking area (with a vault toilet) in the southern part of Nelder Grove is reached after only 0.6 miles. A sign points the way to the *Shadow of the Giants Trail*, a 1.2-mile-long interpretive trail that goes up one side of pretty little Nelder Creek, and then back down the other. John Muir is quoted as saying: *Walk in Sequoia woods at any time of the year and you will say they are the most beautiful and majestic things on earth.* True enough; this trail is indeed pretty at any time of the year, but especially in May and June when the large white flowers of the Pacific dogwood *Cornus nutallii* are in bloom. In early summer, the Western azaleas *Rhododendron occidentale,* growing in moist places along the stream, put on an equally showy display of white or pinkish blossoms. With the cooler days of fall, those same dogwoods that dazzled in the spring now have leaves that turn to shades of pink and rosy red. In the summer, you may also be treated to such wildflowers as the columbine, lupine, and phlox along the trail.

Some call this left branch of the road the "prehistoric" part of Nelder Grove, because long before the coming of white men, Native Americans must have once held Nelder Grove in great awe, too. On a large bare granite outcrop above the creek and just below the Sierra Beauty Tree, one can find several shallow grinding holes where acorns were once pounded into a meal. Nearby, on the banks of Nelder Creek, they would establish a temporary summer camp. There are three other places once occupied by the Southern Miwok Indians; some of these sites may be 4,000 years old.

Look for bedrock mortars on the large flat rock
behind the Sierra Beauty tree.

The "historic" part of Nelder Grove lies to the right of the 'T' intersection. After going only 0.6 miles, the road comes to a small log cabin, the site of the old California No. 2 Sawmill. While the few remaining remnants of the old sawmill were destroyed in the 1922 forest fire, John Hawksworth and his wife Marge spent some twenty summers up here as campground hosts after his retirement from the Forest Service. Having a lot of time on his hands, John located the foundations of the various mill buildings, and took careful measurements. John was a master model builder, and he put that skill to work during the winter months when he patiently, and painstakingly, created a scale model of the mill buildings that once stood at Nelder Grove. (John's model may be seen at the Fresno Flats Historical Park in Oakhurst.)

A short distance beyond the old mill site is the small, but very pleasant Nelder Grove Campground [Elevation 5500'] that has the usual campground amenities, including a host, but no potable water. From this end on Forest Road 6S90, the *Graveyard of the Giants Trail* winds its way for more than a mile through an old growth forest of living Sequoia trees, once mature trees burned in the 1922 fire,

The Bull Buck Tree

and the high stumps of trees felled in the 1880s. Another nearby trail is the *Chimney Tree Trail*, which wanders up the hillside to a Sequoia tree partially burned in the 1922 fire. It has a hole in its base through which a person can walk.

Still another, shorter trail starts at the restrooms in the lower campground and leads to the Bull Buck Tree, once thought to be the largest Sequoia tree in the world, bigger even than the General Sherman Tree in the Giant Forest area of Sequoia National Park. (The two trees are thought to be about the same age, 2700-2800 years old.) This controversy about the "biggest" tree came to a head in 1975, when a team from the American Forestry Association made an "official" measurement of the Bull Buck Tree in front of a crowd of sixty interested observers from the U.S. Forest Service, the National Park Service, the State of California, the Save-The-Redwoods League, and of course, the local press. Careful measurements were taken at a point 4½ feet above the ground by certified engineers. The Bull Buck Tree was found to be 84.2 feet in circumference, as compared with the General Sherman Tree previously measured at 83 feet. The Forest Service supporters were elated, only to have their hopes dashed later when the 274' height of the Sherman Tree beat out the 247' height of the Bull Buck Tree. Clearly, in terms of total volume, the General Sherman Tree is the world's largest living thing. (The world's tallest trees are the Coastal redwoods, and the oldest trees are the nearly 5,000-year-old Bristlecone pines of the Great Basin country.)

Measuring the Bull Buck Tree in 1974
(*Sierra Star* photo)

In spite of the fact that the Forest Service has designated a 1540-acre tract in and around Nelder Grove for special management and protection, all is not well here. The threat of a catastrophic fire threatens the very existence of Nelder Grove more today than at any time in the past 150 years. Studies have shown that the timber cutting of the 1880s was beneficial to the young Sequoia trees that were not cut. With so much of the forest canopy cleared away by the cutting of mature Sequoia, fir, and Sugar pine trees, sunlight was now able to penetrate to the ground, causing many young Sequoias to get a healthy start in life. When Nelder Grove was acquired by the Forest Service in 1928, six years after a disastrous forest fire swept through the grove, the new emphasis was placed on preserving these giant trees and controlling forest fires. In the 85+ years since the last major forest fire swept through here, more trees and brush have grown up and once again the amount of sunlight reaching the new seedlings on the ground is very limited. The Forest Service's success in keeping fire out of Nelder Grove has created another problem.

Normally, foresters like to see no more than twenty tons per acre of duff, brush, and downed wood lying on the forest floor, where it can fuel a forest fire. Yet here today in Nelder Grove accumulations of up to eighty tons per acre are just awaiting ignition. As much as forest rangers would like to clean up the excess fuels in order to make the area more "fire safe," federal budget cuts have deleted the necessary funding. Meanwhile, as more and more fuel accumulates on the ground every year, the potential threat becomes more grave. The fear is that such a fire will not only destroy the young and immature trees, so necessary for the grove's future existence, but that many of the old growth mature trees will also be destroyed.

It's hard to imagine that a tiny seed from small cones
like these could produce such forest giants.

A stump along the Graveyard of the Giants Trail

Side Trip #10
from page 91
The Lewis Creek Trail to
Corlieu Falls and Sugar Pine

**This moderate hike of two miles to the base of the falls
or four miles to Sugar Pine is accessible most of the year.**

Corlieu Falls is a gem of a waterfall, practically within shouting distance
of Highway 41, yet secluded and peacefully hidden away far from the crowds
of summer. Reaching the falls requires a little walk, but the trail is not overly
strenuous and well within the capability of most folks. Even if the falls were not
there, the 3.8-mile-long Lewis Creek Trail, designated a *National Recreational
Trail*, is a worthy destination in its own right. Ideally, hikers should attempt to
come with two vehicles so that one could be left at each end, thus allowing
hikers to walk-through the entire trail without having to double back. Under
such circumstances, the path is easier still by starting at the Sugar Pine end, and
walking all downhill to the Cedar Valley end.

To find this idyllic spot, turn to the right as you come to the stop sign on Sky
Ranch Road at State Route 41. Note your odometer reading and proceed north up
the highway in the direction of Yosemite. Just a little over a hundred yards up the
road, look to the right for the preserved section of the old flume at the entrance
to ECCO (the Episcopal Conference Center).

A preserved section of the Madera Sugar Pine flume
can be seen alongside Highway 41.

After going only 1.2 miles from Road 632, turn to the right again onto the narrow, but paved Cedar Valley Road. Follow this road as it begins a gentle descent into the Lewis Creek drainage. At 1.7 miles, disregard Deer Run Trail going off to the right, and continue straight ahead. At a point 2.3 miles from Road 632, look to the left for a turnout where cars have obviously parked previously. A wooden Forest Service sign indicates this is the Lewis Creek Trail, (officially designated by some romantic type person in the Forest Service as 21E06). For folks who wonder about such things, Lewis Creek derives its name from one Jonathan Lewis, who filed a homestead in what is known as Cedar Valley today. Lewis planted an apple orchard and raised garden vegetables as well as hogs, cattle, donkeys, and horses.

This hiking trail follows Lewis Creek upstream to the site of the great sawmill and lumber camp at Sugar Pine. Corlieu Falls is about half way along the trail.

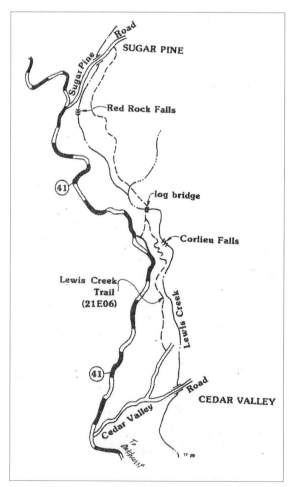

The footpath also follows the route of the V-shaped flume that once floated bundles of cut lumber 54 miles down to Madera. For most of the route, the trail passes through a mixed forest of Incense cedar, Ponderosa pine, Sugar pine, Canyon live oak, and California black oak.

The elevation here at the lower end of the trail is 3,360 feet with the Sugar Pine end at 4,240 feet, for a total elevation gain of 880 feet. This is an average of 231 vertical feet per mile, a fairly easy gradient by any standard. Actually, for most of the walk the gradient is only about 125-150 feet per mile. As you reach the base of Corlieu Falls, the trail becomes more steep as it makes its way to the top of the falls. Once on top, the path levels out again as it follows the stream on up to Sugar Pine.

There is no "best time" to take this trail, because it has its own special charm in every season. Springtime is very nice, because nature puts on a fine wildflower display all along the trail, accentuated by the occasional showy white dogwood blossoms and dazzling streamside displays of Western azaleas. Summer brings on warm temperatures, but the shade offered by the forest canopy is cooling, and the ever-present Lewis Creek invites the hiker to cool off in its rollicking waters. Autumn brings on a peaceful quiet to the woods. The hues of yellow and gold of the turning oak leaves prepare the visitor for the occasional encounter with the bright crimson leaves of the dogwood. Winter, too, offers its own experiences. The lower portion of the trail to the base of the falls is often snow free. The icicles formed along the banks of the creek are a delight to behold.

Corlieu Falls gains its name from Clifford Corlieu, a poet and entrepreneur who operated a small resort here shortly after the Turn of the 20th Century. In those days Highway 41 was not yet built, and Corlieu's guests walked in via the Lewis Creek Trail, either following the flume trail up the from Salt Springs just above Fresno Flats,

Corlieu Falls
(photo by Dan Carter)

or by following the flume down from Sugar Pine. As pretty as the waterfalls were, that was not Corlieu's only attraction. There was also a warm spring on the east side of Lewis Creek from which Corlieu piped warm water to a small five foot square bath house he built on the west side of the stream. One entered the roofless enclosure by a ladder. Nearby, he had also erected some small cabins for use by overnight visitors. In the 1920s, Corlieu further enhanced the amenities of his little resort by installing a water-powered generator so the camp could have electricity.

Clifford Corlieu died in 1929 at the age of 68, and was buried in the place he so much came to love. His grave is on the hillside a short distance down from the parking area off Highway 41 just above the 4,000-foot sign. Upon Corlieu's death, his son-in-law took over the place, staked numerous mining claims, and then tried to sell the claims as cabin sites. The Forest Service did not think this to be a proper use of public land, and revoked the Special Use Permit under which the resort had been operating. In 1965, after years of litigation, the Forest Service succeeded in reasserting their control. They tore the structures down and carried out the debris, leaving Corlieu Falls in a natural state for the public's enjoyment.

Above the falls there is a fork in the trail. One branch makes the short climb up the hill to the west to come out at a parking area on Highway 41 near the 4,000-foot sign and Corlieu's grave. The other branch crosses a log bridge over Lewis Creek, and follows the east bank of the stream on up to Sugar Pine.

The footbridge over Lewis Creek

After hiking about 3½ miles from Cedar Valley, pretty little Red Rock Falls signals that you are about to come to the end of the trail. Suddenly a paved road will be encountered at the lower end of Sugar Pine, once the site of the large mill and associated company town operated by the Sugar Pine Lumber Company between the years 1899 and 1933. Parts of the mill were burned in a 1923 forest fire, and many of the surviving buildings were salvaged when the mill shut down in 1933. Some of the small houses, once occupied by company employees and their families, still remain to this day. While Sugar Pine has a small population of year around residents, most of the old cottages are occupied primarily as summer homes.

Red Rock Falls
(Debby Carter photo)

The Sugar Pine Mill circa 1928
(Fresno Flats Historical Park photo)

Clifford Corlieu near his home
above Lewis Creek
(Fresno Flats Historical Park photo)

Corlieu is still there

Sierra's Call

by
Clifford Corlieu

Give me the mountains,
The glorious mountains,
Whose beauties all come from the snows,
Where nature's hand blesses
The soul with caresses
Of free life and quiet repose.

Where free from all business
And commercial fizziness,
And straight jacket 'ciety rule,
I can eat drink and slouch it,
And not have to couch it
Neath pretense, or be called a fool.

Give me grand Sierra
In county Madera
To live among its great peaks,
With climate that's peeree,
And forest so deery,
And rainbows a-swarm in its creeks.

Where a strenuous hike it
Soon leads you to like it,
For it hardens your corny foot mellows;
Expanding your muscle,
Reducing your bustle,
And makes your lungs work like a bellows.

Where camp fare and clime,
Soon make you feel prime;
Make steely your sinew and bone,
Your muscle and bust
Swell out like the crust
Often an old time dutch oven baked pone.

Hie then to Sierra's mountain
Where joys are beyond your countin;
There fountains of health
And ledges of wealth
Call with favors abounden.

127

Side Trip #11

Bass Lake

Just a few miles east of Highway 41, Bass Lake is a popular vacation spot, certainly worthy of a visit if you have never been there, if not a week's stay. Enjoyable activities in the Bass Lake Recreation Area include picnicking, camping, water-skiing, personal watercraft riding, pleasure boating, fishing, mountain-biking and hiking.

Bass Lake and 4,674' Goat Mountain
(Fresno Flats Historical Park)

Before there ever was a Bass Lake, the tree-lined meadow area across the ridge to the east of Fresno Flats was known as Crane Valley, so named for the great flocks of Sandhill cranes that once nested in the tall grass of the meadow. Willow Creek ran through the little valley throughout the year, and the Western Mono found it to their liking. Archaeological evidence discovered around the basin suggests the area was occupied, at least seasonally, for several hundred years. Perhaps it was inevitable that change would come to this idyllic vale, but change it did. Beginning in April and May of 1851, the Mormon Battalion made camp here while on a punitive expedition chasing renegade Indians. The citizen-soldiers of the Mormon Battalion were soon followed by the establishment of the Board Ranch in Crane Valley. By 1852, men named Reed and Ellis were hard at work on the Board Ranch, hand splitting roofing shakes that they sold in the developing community of North Fork. Using the water from Willow Creek to power his sawmill, George McCullough followed them in the period of 1857 to 1872. He was assisted by a Thomas Winkelman, who, with his wife and nine children, homesteaded land in Crane Valley. Other early sawmills in the area now beneath the waters of Bass Lake include the Dunlap Mill, operating from 1862 to 1867, and the steam-powered Green Mill of 1865 to 1870. An 1891 atlas shows seven ranches in Crane Valley, with a wagon road connecting them with North Fork.

The industrial era came to the area in 1895, when the San Joaquin Electric Company built a powerhouse on Willow Creek to provide electricity to the booming city of Fresno. In 1899-1900, this led to the construction on the stream of a small dam built of dirt, moistened with water and packed by a herd of goats, whose small sharp hooves served to pack it to a cement-like consistency. Subsequently the dam was enlarged in 1905, 1907, and 1910. The resulting creation was today's Bass Lake, a reservoir 4.1 miles long by about a half-mile wide.

The Bass Lake Dam in the 1920s, when the steam trains of the
Minarets and Western Railroad ran across it carrying
logs from Central Camp to the mill at Pinedale.
(Fresno Flats Historical Park photo)

To find this beautiful mountain lake nestled among the pine forest, reset your trip odometer to zero at the Mountain House Restaurant, at the intersection of Highway 41 and Road 222. Take Road 222 eastward as it makes the gradual 2½-mile ascent to Chepo Saddle. Upon crossing the divide, you leave the Lewis Creek/Fresno River watershed on the west, and enter the Willow Creek watershed on the east. Once over the saddle, the road descends nearly a mile to an important road junction where your trip odometer should now be reading 3.4 miles. Here Road 274 goes straight ahead, while Road 222 turns off to the right. By either fork, North Fork is about 12 miles to the south. For our present purposes, let's stay to the right on Road 222. After going only 0.3 miles, another important road junction is reached. Again Road 222 goes off to the right, while Road 432 goes to the left. Again, either branch will take you along the shore of Bass Lake, to ultimately reach North Fork in about 12 miles. The choice of route is yours.

The southwest shore of Bass Lake via Road 222:

At 4.2 miles the Crane Valley Group Camp is passed on the right, followed immediately by the Bass Lake Forest Station, now containing the offices of the concessionaire operating the local campgrounds. On the left side of Road 222 is the Recreation Point Group Picnic area. A quarter-mile further on the 38-unit Denver Church Picnic Area is also on the left. The Little Denver Church Picnic Area follows it along the shore. All of these day use facilities have running water, flush toilets, and offer easy access to the lake.

Trailhead parking for the mile-long *Way of the Mono* self-guiding interpretative trail is at the 4.8-mile point. This easy footpath winds its way up the hillside, with stations along the trail that tell about the life of the Native Americans who occupied this area prior to the coming of the white man.

The Pines Picnic Area is on the left at 5.3 miles, followed in ¼-mile by The Forks Resort at the intersection of Roads 222 and 426. Prior to World War II, this little resort consisted of a dock and boathouse, a small store, and three rental cabins that dated back to 1900, when occupied by construction workers building the dam. When Robert Miller bought the property in 1941, he had a more ambitious vision. Unfortunately, his hard work and dreams went up in smoke two days before Labor Day of 1949, when the store burned to the ground. Miller rebuilt and the Forks came back the following year stronger than ever. In the well over half a century since, thousands of people have enjoyed the rustic ambiance of the cabins, purchased ice, picnic and camping supplies from the store, and enjoyed a famous "Forks burger" and chips. Gasoline is available at the store for motorists, and at the end of the dock for boaters. Boat rentals are also available.

The Forks Resort, circa 1950
(from the authors' collection)

130

Just beyond The Forks Resort, on Road 222, is the 31-unit Forks Campground, offering running water and flush toilets. One of two hiking trails to the now-closed fire lookout on the summit of 4,674' Goat Mountain begins at the south edge of the campground. It is said that the owner of the goats that helped build the dam turned them loose when construction was completed, and they strayed to the mountain that towers over Bass Lake, giving it the name of "Goat Mountain."

At the 7.3-mile point from Highway 41 is another even larger campground, the 113-unit Lupine-Cedar Bluff Campground, which also has running water and flush toilets. Across the road is the Lakeside Picnic Area. Within the next mile, there are two more picnic areas, Pine Point and Rocky Point. The 63-unit Spring Cove Campground (running water and flush toilets) is at the 8.1-mile point. Here, too, begins the Spring Cove trail, an alternate hiking trail that climbs up to the Goat Mountain fire lookout tower and the spectacular panoramic view of the lake and the mountains beyond.

Operated by the Pacific Gas & Electric Company Employees Association, the privately owned Camp Wishon Cove occupies a little cove at the 8.5-mile point. Around the next bend of the road at 8.7 miles is Miller's Landing, another lakeside resort and marina offering cabins, a restaurant, store, gasoline, boat rentals and a dockside marine refueling station. This friendly resort and store goes back to the pre-World War I era, when Bass Lake first became a popular summer recreation destination. Over the years, the store has changed hands and names many times. Known variously as the Lake View Store, McDougald's Lake View Store, McDougalds Wishon Cove Resort, it is now Miller's Landing. The little cove got its very own post office in 1923 to serve the workers of the Minarets & Western Railroad living nearby. That post office was named Wishon, California, after Albert Graves Wishon, the General Manager of the San Joaquin Power Company who, at the Turn of the 20th Century, brought hydro-electrially-generated power from the mountains to Fresno and the surrounding communities in the San Joaquin Valley. The small Wishon post office remained open until 1986, when it fell to the bean counter's ax. The last thirty postal patrons now have to go to The Pines Village to buy their stamps. Nevertheless, incoming mail to local residents still carries Wishon's exclusive Zip Code, 93669.

The last of Bass Lake's Forest Service campgrounds, the 60-unit Wishon Point Campground is 9.0 miles from Highway 41. It, too, has running water and flush toilets. Nearby at the dam is the public boat ramp.

Below the dam, it is only 5½ miles to North Fork via Road 222.

The northeast shore of Bass Lake via Roads, 432, 434, and 274:
By choosing the left fork, Road 432 (North Shore Road) passes through the lake's residential area stretched out along the next two miles of the northeast shore. Many of these residences were built in the World War I era as resort cabins.

In recent years, however, land previously leased by PG&E to cabin owners has been purchased outright. With full ownership of the land, lenders were willing to make substantial home loans, and property values began to skyrocket. Since the 1970s, more and more of those little 1,000-square-foot cabins have been torn down to be replaced by very nice homes, some of which are valued in excess of one million dollars.

At the 4.5-mile point from Highway 41, the North Shore Road makes a sharp turn to the right as it crosses Willow Creek over a concrete bridge. This was once the site of "The Falls," the second oldest resort at Bass Lake. It began in 1916. Although destroyed by fire in 1922, by flood in 1950, and by heavy snow in 1955, The Falls always came back, until 1969 that is, when the Forest Service lease expired. The building was torn down, and the land returned to public use. For more than a half-century, The Falls was noted for its very popular Saturday night dances, with teens on the upper floor, and adults in the bar below.

"The Falls" was a well-known entertainment hot spot in the 1950s.
(Photo by Jack Gyer, *Sierra Star* Collection)

A short distance beyond the bridge is the parking area for the Falls Beach, one of two popular day use areas on the northeast side of the lake. The Willow Creek Trail can be accessed across the road from here. Angel Falls and Devil's Slide and a variety of quiet spots and scenic views are to be found along this challenging hiking trail. While the breathtaking waterfalls are spectacular, Willow Creek presents dangers in its extremely slippery rocks and swirling pools. **Be Careful, and stay on the trail.**

At the 5.8-mile point from Highway 41, Road 432 comes to The Pines Village, the center of summer life at Bass Lake for the last 100 years. The resort offices and lobby burned in 1962, together with the adjoining, restaurant, grocery store, soda fountain, bar and post office. All were quickly rebuilt. Today there is a fully stocked market, several places to eat, a post office, docks and a boat launch ramp (marine fueling facilities) and offices where cabin rentals can be booked. The marina offers for rent personal watercraft and boats of all kinds, including party boats. The Pines is also home to Ducey's, an upscale hostelry offering rooms with a scenic view and fine dining.

The original Pines Resort clubhouse, circa 1917
(photo from the authors' collection)

The Pines Village before the 1962 fire
(Fresno Flats Historical Park photo)

Road 432 ends at The Pines, but you can easily go on to North Fork by turning left at the gas station onto Road 434, then right again onto Road 274 (Malum Ridge Road). It is only ten miles from The Pines Village to North Fork.

Side Trip #12
from page 93
Fresno Flats Historical Park

The last of our optional side trips takes the visitor to the Fresno Flats Historical Park, where a number of local historic buildings have been relocated and preserved. A stop at the museum complex is well worth the hour it takes to tour the facility.

At the traffic signal for the intersection of Highway 41 and Road 426 (Crane Valley Road) next to the "Talking Bear," go east on Road 426, passing the Rite Aid drug store on the right. Almost immediately, the road crosses the concrete bridge over the Fresno River.

In spite of its name, the Fresno River flows nowhere near Fresno. During periods of high water, such as during the spring snowmelt, the Fresno River flows some 35 miles to the south, through the City of Madera, and another 35 miles beyond to eventually flow into the San Joaquin River near the town of Firebaugh. One might reasonably ask then: If the Fresno River does not flow through the City of Fresno, why is it called the "Fresno River?" Keep in mind that this area was first settled in the 1850s, when its residents raised garden vegetables, fruit, and meat to feed the hungry miners in Coarsegold and other nearby mining camps. It was the early settlers who named the Fresno River, and they called their small community "Fresno Flats," after the ash trees growing along the riverbank. ("Fresno" is the Spanish word for ash tree.) At that time, the present day City of Fresno was nothing except open grasslands. Fresno's humble beginnings did not start until 1872, when, while extending its rails south towards Visalia, the Central Pacific Railroad created a siding, and named it Fresno Station, presumably because ash trees were growing there, as well. Thus, because Fresno Flats existed nearly twenty years before Fresno had its most humble beginnings, the good folks of Oakhurst wonder why the railroad chose the name "Fresno" for their little whistle-stop, when they were 25 miles from the nearest point on the Fresno River! (Predictably, confusion in the two names resulted and, in 1912, the citizenry of Fresno Flats wanted to break completely away from the "Fresno" name. Accordingly, they changed the name of their community to Oakhurst.)

Proceed 0.4 miles to the next traffic signal, which is at the intersection of Road 426 (Crane Valley Road) and Road 427 (School Road); turn left onto School Road. Proceed north another 0.4 miles, and you will see the gate leading to Fresno Flats Historical Park on the left. Ample off-street parking is provided. (If you come to Indian Springs Road on the left, you have gone about 100 feet too far.)

We suggest that you start your visit at the Nathan Sweet Museum, and work your way counter clockwise around the grounds. You might ask in the museum to see if a volunteer docent is available to show you around.

The structure housing the museum was built in 1874 as a schoolhouse. It is one of the oldest buildings in Oakhurst, and was the second school in what is Madera County today. In later years, it served as a justice court, county offices, and a public library. The structure originally stood at the corner of Highway 41 and Road 426 (Crane Valley Road) now occupied by the Rite Aid drug store. The museum has exhibits displaying various aspects of local history. It also houses a small gift shop.

Next to the museum is the Cunningham School, opened in 1913 in what is now Nipinnawasee, a few miles to the north on Highway 49. This was the only building in that little community to survive the Harlow Fire of 1961. It was spared by the fact that the grounds around it had been worn bare by 50 years of children running around the playground. Today, the building is used by the Sierra Historic Sites Association for social events and as a meeting hall.

The next structure encountered in our circuit is the wooden Fresno Flats Jail. Next to the jail is Taylor log house. With an open breezeway between the two halves, this two-room log house was built in 1869 by William Taylor for his wife Margaret. The design was common in Arkansas, Tennessee, and Kentucky in the mid 1800s. The room at one end was the "family room," where the cooking was done and where the Taylor family gathered for meals. The other room, across the open "dogtrot," was the adult's bedroom, as well as mom's sewing room. The children slept in the unheated loft accessible by a ladder. William died accidentally in 1881. The cabin was originally located about ½-mile from here, and moved to this site in 1981.

Built in 1869, the Taylor log house is the
oldest surviving structure in Oakhurst.

Continuing our circuit, the next structure is an open pole barn containing various horse-drawn wagons and buggies, next to an old barn, now containing old printing equipment. The blacksmith's shop and then the Raymond Jail follow. This wooden structure was more of a holding cell than a jail. Up to fourteen prisoners could he held here pending transfer to the main county jail in Madera.

Behind the Raymond Jail is the Dupzyk family barn, built in 1914. Originally standing about a mile east of here, it was painstakingly dismantled and reassembled here. In front of the barn is a section of the wooden flume that once carried cut lumber from the mill in Sugar Pine 54 miles down through Oakhurst to the railroad in Madera.

We have saved the best for last, the two story Laramore home. The house was built by Robert and Catherine Laramore in 1878, shortly after they moved to Fresno Flats. At the time, it was located about a half-mile to the south on Fresno Flats' main street (now Road 425B). Robert Laramore ran the general store in Fresno Flats, and helped with the original construction of the lumber flume to Madera. He was killed in a run-away carriage accident in 1896. The house was given to the museum's parent organization, the Sierra Historic Sites Association, in 1973 and moved here in 1975. Hopefully at the time of your visit, there will be a docent who can tell you about the interior that is decorated with furnishings of the times. The upstairs wallpaper is original.

The Laramore house was built in 1878
and is furnished with period pieces.

The Fresno Flats Historical Park is operated by volunteers of the Sierra Historic Sites Association. No fixed admission is charged, but donations are certainly appreciated.

References

Annon., *History of Madera County*, Madera CA: Madera County Board of Education, 1939.

_____, *Teledyne Tungsten Strawberry Mine,* information booklet on the Strawberry Mine for mine visitors, Fresno CA: Teledyne Tungsten Inc., 1982.

_____, As *We Were Told*, Coarsegold CA: Coarsegold Historical Society, 1990.

_____, *Madera County 1883-1983*, Madera CA: Madera Newspapers Inc., 1993.

_____, *Sierra National Forest, Centennial Celebration,* Putney Ranch, North Fork CA: USFS, October 5, 2005.

Abrams, Paul, 'Fishing with a view at Mammoth Pool', *Sierra Star*, Oakhurst CA: July 1, 2005.

Barnes, Dwight, 'Popular 22 Mile House: 22 miles from where?', *Sierra Star,* Oakhurst CA: February 14, 2001.

_____, *Miners, Lumberjacks, and Cowboys*, Oakhurst CA: Sierra Historic Sites Ass'n, 2001.

_____, 'Wide-Awake Ranch is part of our Wild West', *Sierra Star*, Oakhurst CA: February 13, 2002.

_____, 'Eastern Madera County's own grove of Sequoia trees', *Sierra Star*, Oakhurst CA: April 17, 2002.

Bender, Marguerite, 'The Big Trees at Bass Lake – Protection Plans Eyed', *The Fresno Bee*, Fresno CA: July 16, 1978.

Birman, Joseph H., *Glacial Geology Across the Crest of the Sierra Nevada, California*, Special Paper 75, New York NY: Geological Society of America, 1964.

Brown, Francis, L., 'Obsidian Tells A Story', *Sierra Star*, Oakhurst CA: September 23, 1981.

_____, 'Archeological dig by Highway 41 turned up some interesting things', *The North Fork Journal*, North Fork CA: July 27, 1989.

_____, 'Little Table Mountain', *Sierra Star*, Oakhurst CA: January 23, 1992.

_____, 'A visit with the living and dead giants of the forest', *The North Fork Journal*, North Fork CA: December 2, 1993.

_____, 'Grass Lands of Eastern Madera County', *Sierra Star*, Oakhurst CA: May 23, 1996.

_____, 'The Crane Valley and Mammoth Wagon Road became the French Trail', *Sierra Star*, Oakhurst CA: Aug. 22, 1996.

Clough, Charles W., *Madera,* Madera CA: Madera County Historical Society, 1968.

DeGraff, Jerome V., Internal Forest Service report to Minarets District Ranger on the origin of Globe Rock, April 26, 1987.

_____, Internal Forest Service report to Minarets District Ranger on the origin of Arch Rock, June 26, 1987.

Dunavan, Volney, 'Protecting Our Forests - Bark Beetles', *Sierra Star*, Oakhurst CA: Jan. 23, 2004.

Everest, Irl, (District Ranger) *The Nelder Grove Story*, Undated USFS handout.

Fontana, Cyndee, 'A Fork in the Road', *The Fresno Bee,* Fresno CA: May 8, 2003.

Gudde, Erwin G., *California Gold Camps*, Berkeley, Los Angeles, and London: University of California Press, 1976.

Hill, Mary, *Geology of the Sierra Nevada*, Berkeley, Los Angeles, London: University of California Press, 1975.

Huber, N. King, *Geologic Map of the Shuteye Peak Quadrangle Sierra Nevada, California*, Map GQ-782, Washington DC: U.S. Geological Survey, 1968.

_____, Paul C. Bateman, and Clark Wahrhafrig, *Geological Map of Yosemite National Park and Vicinity, California*, Map I-1874, Washington DC: U.S. Geological Survey, 1989.

Johnson, Hank, *Thunder in the Mountains*, 2nd. ed., Corona del Mar CA: Trans-Anglo Books, 1958.

_____, *Rails to the Minarets,* Corona del Mar CA: Trans-Anglo Books, 1980.

Jones, Johnny, Transcript of oral history interview with Dwight Barnes, Oakhurst CA: Fresno Flats Historical Park, October 24, 1990.

_____, *Following the Bells,* as told to Dwight Barnes, Oakhurst CA: Dwight Barnes, 1994.

Kelley, Kathy, 'The Forks Resort observes its 46th anniversary in '87', *Sierra Star*, Oakhurst CA: April 3, 1986.

Klette, Bud, 'The History of North Fork', *North Fork Journal*, North Fork CA: published in serial parts from July 25, 1963, to October 25, 1963.

Klette, William, 'Fine Gold Gulch: Whiskey And Cards Played A Role', *The Fresno Bee,* Fresno CA: April 23, 1971.

Logan, C.A., 'Mines and Mineral Resources of Madera County', *California Journal of Mines and Geology,* Vol. 46 No. 4, San Francisco CA: California Division of Mines, October 1960.

LeFevre, Michael, *Sierra Vista Scenic Byway, Development and Interpretive Plan,* Sierra National Forest, March 1991.

Mackie, Ron, 'Bull Buck Tree is not the biggest tree but is beautiful', *Sierra Star*, Oakhurst CA: April 23, 1987.

_____, 'Most people find little to say in the praise of the Digger Pine', *Sierra Star*, Oakhurst CA: July 18, 1987.

_____, 'The Great French Trail Mystery', *Sierra Star*, Oakhurst CA: September 1990.

Mason, Ruth & Bill, *History of Fresno Flats*, Oakhurst CA: self published, 1997 edition.

Mitchell, Roger, *High Sierra SUV Trails, Volume II – The Western Slope*, Oakhurst CA: Track & Trail Publications, 2002.

Nokleberg, Warren J., *Stratigraphy and Structure of the Strawberry Mine Roof Pendant Central Sierra Nevada, California*, Professional Paper 1154, Washington DC: U.S. Geological Survey, 1981.

Peck, Dallas L., *Geologic Map of the Merced Peak Quadrangle, Central Sierra Nevada, California*, Map GQ-1531, Washington DC: U.S. Geological Survey, 1980.

Prusek, Denice, 'A view of the past at Nelder Grove', *Sierra Star*, Oakhurst CA: July 13, 1989.

Reed, Charles, *Along The Forks of Willow Creek*, unpublished manuscript, 1983.

Rees, Lacy, 'Nelder Grove', *Sierra Star*, Oakhurst CA: July 19 & 25, 2000.

138

_____ 'Battersons Part of Mountain Area History', *Sierra Star*, Oakhurst CA: July 25, 2003.

Rose, Gene, 'Which Tree is the Mightiest of All?', *The Fresno Bee*, Fresno CA: Sept. 5, 1975.

_____, *Sierra Centennial*, Auberry CA: Three Forests Interpretive Association, 1993.

_____, *The San Joaquin, A River Betrayed*, Clovis CA: Word Dancer Press, 2000.

Smith, Judy Edwina, *Sierra National Forest, A History of the Bass Lake District to 1930*, Masters degree thesis, Fresno CA: California State University Fresno, November 1983.

Storer, Tracey I., and Robert L. Usinger, *Sierra Nevada Natural History*, Berkeley, Los Angeles, and London: University of California Press, 1963.

Tucker, Trudie, 'Added Protection - Scouts, adults join forces to keep historic Nelder Grove cabin safe', *Sierra Star*, Oakhurst CA: Oct. 17, 2001.

Wagnon, Kenneth, 'Charles and Bettie O'Neal', *The Madera County Historian*, Vol. IV No. 2, Madera CA: October 1975.

Ward, Earlene, 'One day of hard travel brought people from Fresno to Coarsegold in early days', *Sierra Star*, Oakhurst CA: Dec. 14, 1985.

_____, 'Wishon Post Office is Closed', *Sierra Star*, Oakhurst CA: April 3, 1986.

Willard, Dwight, *A Guide to the Sequoia Groves of California*, Yosemite CA: The Yosemite Association, 2000.

Index

Index

Index

142

Index

144

Index

About the Authors

The authors are no strangers to the Sierra Nevada landscape they write about. Roger has walked down the spine of the Sierra Nevada from Lake Tahoe to Kernville, long before backpacking was the "In" thing to do. With a college degree in Geology, and a passion for photography, he has been writing outoor books and magazine articles since the early 1960s. Loris spent her childhood summers at the family home at Bass Lake, and has a keen interest in history and nature. Residents of Oakhurst for nearly 30 years, their mountaintop home is 1,000 feet above the community. Every morning when they rise, they are greeted with a view of Fresno Dome.

The Mitchells are actively involved in preserving local history at the Research Library of the Fresno Flats Historical Park. Roger is the curator of historical photos, while Loris works in the library's archives.

Roger and Loris have travelled extensively throughout the world, but now spend most of their time closer to home exploring back roads and byways. They enjoy sharing their adventures through their writing, and hope to inspire their readers to explore these wonderful places. Look for their SUV Trail Guides and future new titles.

146

Other Guidebooks from TRACK & TRAIL PUBLICATIONS

High Sierra SUV Trails Series

High Sierra SUV Trails Vol. I
The East Side

35 rough road adventures with excursions out of Reno, Truckee, South Lake Tahoe, Markleeville, Bridgeport, Lee Vining, Mammoth Lakes, Bishop, Big Pine, Independence, and Lone Pine.

240 pages   **$16.95**

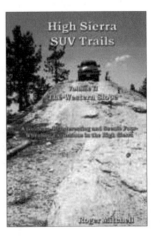

High Sierra SUV Trails Vol. II
The Western Slope

40 rough road adventures with excursions out of Auburn, Foresthill, Placerville, Jackson, Angels Camp, Sonora, Pinecrest, Mariposa, Oakhurst, Shaver Lake, Mono Hot Springs, Kings Canyon National Park, and Kernville.

272 pages   **$18.95**

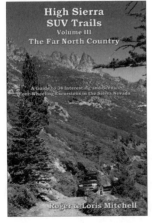

High Sierra SUV Trails Vol. III
The Far North Country

34 rough road adventures with excursions out of Auburn, Truckee, Grass Valley-Nevada City, Downieville, Sierra City, Oroville, La Porte, Quincy, Portola, Reno, and Susanville.

304 pages   **$19.95**

Look for them at your favorite bookstore or order them online at
TRACKANDTRAILPUBLICATIONS.COM

Other Guidebooks from TRACK & TRAIL PUBLICATIONS

Death Valley SUV Trails

46 rough road adventures with excursions out of Furnace Creek Ranch, Stovepipe Wells, Scotty's Castle, Beatty, Shoshone, Big Pine, Panamint Springs, Ballarat, and Trona.

322 pages   **$19.95**

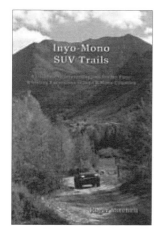

Inyo-Mono SUV Trails

40 rough road adventures with excursions out of Bridgeport, Lee Vining, Mammoth Lakes, Bishop, Big Pine, Independence, Lone Pine, and Olancha.

304 pages   **$19.95**

Southern California SUV Trails Vol. I
The Western Mojave Desert

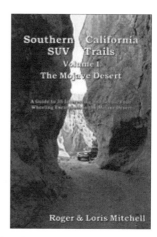

32 rough road adventures with excursions out of Ridgecrest, Randsburg, Mojave, Boron-Kramer Junction, Victorville, and Barstow.

304 pages   **$19.95**

Look for them at your favorite bookstore or order them online at
TRACKANDTRAILPUBLICATIONS.COM

148

Other Guidebooks from TRACK & TRAIL PUBLICATIONS

Great Basin SUV Trails Series

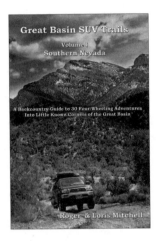

Great Basin SUV Trails Vol. I
Southern Nevada

32 rough road adventures with excursions out of Las Vegas, Boulder City, Searchlight, Laughlin, Pahrump, and Beatty.

272 pages   **$19.95**

Great Basin SUV Trails Vol. II
Southwestern Nevada

34 rough road adventures with excursions out of Beatty, Goldfield, Tonopah, Bishop, Mina, and Hawthorne.

304 pages   **$1.95**

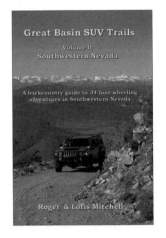

Look for them at your favorite bookstore or order them online at
TRACKANDTRAILPUBLICATIONS.COM

These publications may also be ordered directly from the publisher. Please add appropriate sales tax (CA residents only) and Media Rate shipping of $2.75 for the first book and $1.00 for each additional book. (For Priority Mail: $4.25 for first book and $1.00 for each additional book.)

Send your check to:
TRACK AND TRAIL PUBLICATIONS
P.O. Box 1247
Oakhurst, CA 93644

Notes

Notes

Notes

Notes